THIS
BOOK

belongs to

JONATHAN
KOCHEN

THE
ILLUSTRATED
JEWISH
BIBLE
FOR
CHILDREN

THE ILLUSTRATED JEWISH BIBLE FOR CHILDREN

Foreword by Rabbi Joseph Potasnik

Stories retold by
SELINA HASTINGS

Illustrated by
ERIC THOMAS
and
AMY BURCH

DK PUBLISHING, INC.

A DK PUBLISHING BOOK

Art Editor Shirley Gwillym

Project Editor Marie Greenwood

Senior Editor Emma Johnson

Designer Sarah Cowley

Additional design by
Heather Blackham, Muffy Dodson

Production Ruth Cobb, Marguerite Fenn

Managing Editor Susan Peach

Managing Art Editor Jacquie Gulliver

US Editor B. Alison Weir

Editor's Note
The dates listed in this book are chronicled BCE, meaning
"Before the Common Era," and CE, meaning "Common
Era." However, much of the Christian world uses BC
("Before Christ") and AD ("Anno Domini" or "In the year
of the Lord") to designate eras.

CONSULTANTS

Religious Consultants
Rabbi Joseph Potasnik
Reverend John Glover
Sister K. C. Young
Mary Evans
Jenny Nemko
Reverend Stephen Motyer
Bernadette Chapman
Father Philip Walshe

Educational Consultant
Geoffrey Marshall-Taylor

Historical Consultant
Jonathan Tubb, Western Asiatic Department,
British Museum, London

2 4 6 8 10 9 7 5 3 1

Published in the United States in 1997 by
DK Publishing, Inc.
95 Madison Avenue
New York, New York 10016

Visit us on the World Wide Web at http://www.dk.com

The Children's Illustrated Bible
Copyright © 1994
Dorling Kindersley Limited, London
Text copyright © 1994 Selina Hastings
The right of Selina Hastings to be identified as the Author of this Work has been asserted by her in accordance with
the Copyright Designs and Patents Act 1988.

ISBN 0-7894-2063-5

A catalog record is available from the Library of Congress

Reproduced by Colourscan, Singapore

Printed and bound in the U.S.A. by RR Donnelley & Son's, Roanoke, Virginia

Foreword
by Rabbi Joseph Potasnik
Congregation Mount Sinai, Brooklyn Heights, New York

"Why do I have to learn stories written so many years ago?" I often hear that question from young people studying the Bible. The best answer I can offer is that we live those stories today. Issues such as family strife, sibling rivalry, the conflict of conscience and convenience, and coping with rejection are timeless themes that need timely answers. When God denied Moses entry into the Promised Land, He was teaching us that we never attain all of our aspirations.

The Hebrew Bible is not only the historical birth certificate of the Jewish people but also a blueprint for human living. Judaism professes that belief is measured by behavior. Thus much of the Bible contains moral mandates known as *Mitzvot*, or commandments. It is not enough to speak of charity, one has to be charitable. It is not enough to lecture about honesty, one has to live honestly. The more we read the Bible the better we realize that there is a living lesson plan that allows us to learn from the past in order to live more meaningfully in the present.

When President Woodrow Wilson offered his thirteen-point peace plan to end World War I, one of his elders remarked, "Mr President, you are more stringent than Moses. He only had ten points in the commandments."
To which Wilson responded, "If only the world would keep the ten there would be no need for the thirteen!"

When I studied at the seminary, I learned that the Bible has much quotation but much more interpretation. The beauty of the Bible is that it invites human interpretation in which we learn from each other. In all religions the word "we" is far more important than "I," or as my mother told me there is no "I" in the word "team." Thus, all interpretations are equally important and enhance the beauty of the Bible. The story is told of a father who was watching *The Ten Commandments* on television. As the Egyptians were pursuing the Jewish people, the young boy became horrified.
"Dad, this is horrible, those people fleeing Egypt are not going to make it alive."
"Don't worry, son," said the father, "you will see how God will save them and the Red Sea will become dry land and a safe path."
"Dad, have you seen this before?"

We can read the stories several times, and the more we learn them, the more we live them.

CONTENTS

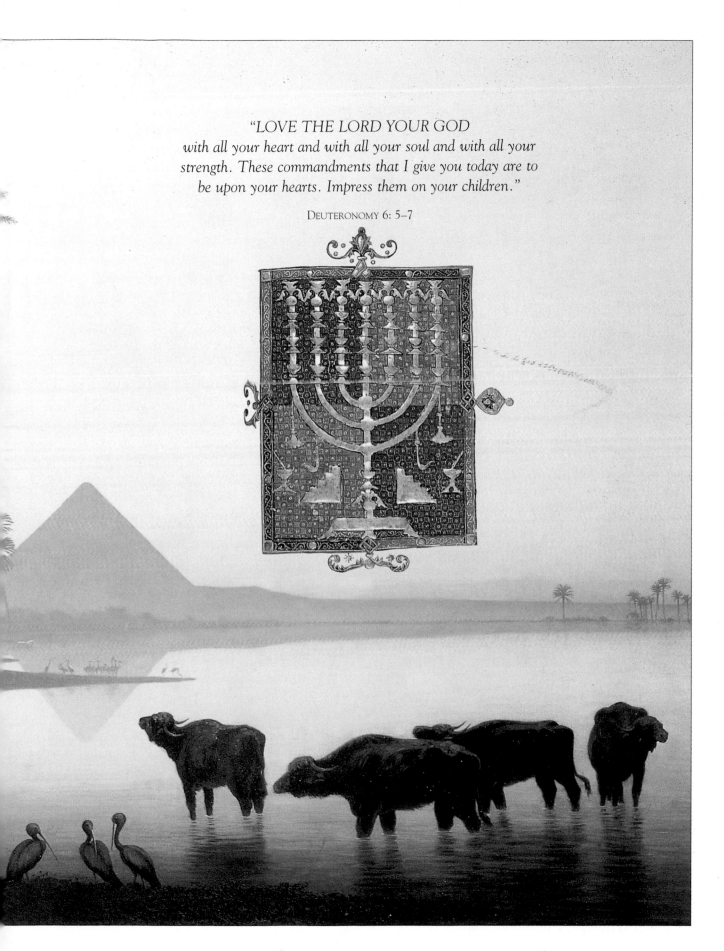

"LOVE THE LORD YOUR GOD
with all your heart and with all your soul and with all your
strength. These commandments that I give you today are to
be upon your hearts. Impress them on your children."

DEUTERONOMY 6: 5–7

Introduction to the Bible

MEDIEVAL BIBLE
A decorative page from an 8th-century Bible in the Royal Library in Stockholm.

THE BIBLE IS A collection of books written by different people during more than 1,000 years and dating from about 1450 BCE. It is divided into two main parts, the Old Testament (or Hebrew Testament) and the New Testament.

The Old Testament books are the Scriptures, or sacred writings, of the Jewish people. They give an account of the people of ancient Israel over many centuries. By contrast, the New Testament, which consists of writings about Jesus and his first followers, covers a period of about 60 or 70 years. Both the Old and New Testaments make up the Christian Bible.

There are 66 books in the Bible. It is often said that it is more like a library because there are so many kinds of writing in it. For example, there are books containing laws, history, poetry, wise sayings or proverbs, diaries, and letters.

The Old Testament
The 39 books of the Old Testament have guided the Jewish people throughout their history. These are the Scriptures which Jesus read. For Jews, the most important part is the Torah – the first five books of the Bible. The word "Torah" means "teaching." The five books are Genesis, Exodus, Leviticus, Numbers, and Deuteronomy. Christians call this the "Pentateuch," a Greek word meaning "five books."

Each Sabbath Jewish congregations listen to a part of the Torah being read from scrolls in the synagogue. It takes a year of weekly readings to go from the beginning to the end. On the day when the last part of the Torah is reached and Genesis chapter one is due to be read again, there is a celebration called *Simchat Torah*, the "rejoicing of the law." A procession dances around the synagogue carrying the Torah scrolls high in thanksgiving.

In Christian services passages from the Old Testament are often read. The stories are considered important by Christians because of what can be learned from them about God, about others, and about themselves.

The Five Books of Moses
The Torah is special to Jews because its books contain God's words given through Moses to the Hebrew people, their ancestors. The Torah is sometimes referred to as "The Five Books of Moses" because of this. Its stories, songs, prayers, and laws teach about God and what he promises to his people and expects from them.

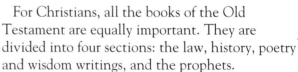

On Mount Sinai, Moses received God's laws.

For Christians, all the books of the Old Testament are equally important. They are divided into four sections: the law, history, poetry and wisdom writings, and the prophets.

At first the words of the earliest books of the Old Testament were passed on by one generation repeating them to the next. Eventually they were written down in the Hebrew language on parchment, which is made from animal skin. Each word was copied carefully by a scribe, as it is today.

A rabbi, or teacher, studies the words of the Torah.

A Jewish boy becomes Bar-Mitvah at the age of 13.

The Torah is studied by young Jews from an early age. When a Jewish boy reaches the age of 13 he becomes *Bar-Mitzvah*, which means "a son of the commandment." He is now a Jewish adult and, on the Sabbath after his birthday, he can read from the Torah in the synagogue. A Jewish girl becomes *Bat-Mitzvah* (daughter of the commandment) at the age of 12. In many synagogues she can also read from the Torah.

The Dead Sea Scrolls

In 1947 a shepherd boy came across some ancient scrolls in caves near the Dead Sea: they were fragments of all the books of the Old Testament, except for Esther, and had probably been written about the time of Jesus. It is thought that they came from the monastery at Qumran and were hidden in the caves by a group of Jews called the Essenes. The discovery showed how accurately scribes had copied these special words throughout the centuries.

Psalm 119 verse 105 explains why the Old Testament is so important to Jews and Christians. The writer says to God, "Thy word is a lamp unto my feet and a light unto my path."

DISCOVERY
The Dead Sea Scrolls, stored in pottery jars, were found in caves at Qumran (below). Some of the fragments date back to the 2nd century BCE

THE OLD TESTAMENT

In the beginning
God created the
heaven
and the earth.

GENESIS 1·1

THE OLD TESTAMENT

MOST OF THE EVENTS OF THE Old Testament take place in a small area to the east of the Mediterranean Sea. From ancient times people have lived and traveled along a strip of land known as the "fertile crescent", which stretches from Egypt, through Canaan and Mesopotamia to Babylonia. There was enough water in this area to enable them to grow crops and graze animals. Many great civilizations have thrived here, and down the centuries there has been much fighting to control the land.

Canaan, the "promised land," where the Israelites flourished, is only about 150 miles (230 km) from north to south. It contains many different types of scenery, including plains and river valleys

suitable for farming, lakes, hills, and rocky desert. The highest mountains are over 3,280 ft (1,000 m) high; the lowest point, at the Dead Sea, is 1,300 ft (400 m) below sea level.

The vegetation of Canaan in biblical times would have been different in many ways from that found today. When the Israelites entered Canaan, much of the hilly ground was covered by woods and forests. Since then many of these have disappeared, cut down and used for building and fuel. In recent years, however, trees have been planted in several areas and there are intensive irrigation projects under way to encourage the desert to "blossom as the rose" (Isaiah, chapter 35).

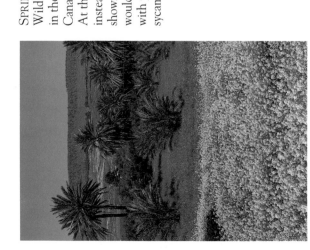

SPRING FIELDS
Wild flowers, like the ones in the photograph, grew in Canaan in biblical times. At that time, however, instead of the palm trees shown here, the landscape would have been covered with poplar, oak, and sycamore trees.

MAP OF CANAAN

Sea of Galilee
Plain of Jezreel
Jezreel
Mt. Carmel
Shunem
Mt. Gilboa
Samaria
ISRAEL
Shiloh
Bethel
Jerusalem
Bethlehem
Hebron
JUDAH
Kerith Brook
Jabesh-gilead
R. Jabbok
Shittim
Jericho
Wilderness of Judah
En-gedi
Mt. Nebo
Sodom and Gomorrah
Dead Sea
R. Jordan
Mediterranean Sea
Beersheba

Nineveh
Jonah and the Great Fish
River Tigris
River Euphrates
MESOPOTAMIA
BABYLONIA
Tower of Babel
Babylon
Ur

Haran
Jacob meets Rachel
SYRIAN DESERT

Lebanon Mts.
Sidon
Tyre
Samaria
Jericho
Jerusalem
CANAAN
Mediterranean Sea
Dead Sea
MOAB
JORDAN
EDOM
NEGEV DESERT
SINAI
Mt. Sinai
The Commandments
Burning Bush
Bitter Lakes
GOSHEN
Rameses
Succoth
Moses in the Bulrushes
River Nile
EGYPT
MIDIAN
Queen of Sheba
ARABIAN DESERT
Red Sea

THE RED SEA
In the story of the Exodus, God divided this narrow body of water so that the Israelites could escape from the Egyptian army.

15

Abraham

IN ONE IMPORTANT way the people of Israel (the Hebrews) were different from others. Instead of many gods, they believed that there was only one God, a divine God. The Bible tells how God made this special promise, or covenant, with Abraham and his descendants, the people of Israel: "I will establish my covenant as an everlasting covenant between me and you, and your descendants after you, to be your God."

On Mount Sinai, God gave to Moses the main laws which the people were to follow: these "Ten Commandments," as they are called, are about ways of honoring God and treating others. There were also laws, or rules, covering many aspects of daily life from marriage to owning property. The Israelites believed that you could worship God not just in prayers and services, but by the way you lived your daily life.

The Ark of the Covenant

The Ten Commandments were written on two pieces of stone and were very precious to the Israelites. They kept them in a golden box called the "Ark of the Covenant." The Ark was also important to them, because it reminded them of God's covenant that he would be with them.

Because the people of Israel spent many years traveling before they found a place to settle, they made a portable tent, or "tabernacle," which they could set up anywhere. The Ark was kept in this tent, and in the area around it sacrifices and prayers were made each day to God. This was the most important place of worship for the Israelites.

The priests carry the box containing the Ten Commandments.

The tabernacle measured 45 feet (14 m) long, 13 feet (4 m) wide, and 16 feet (5 m) high. It was made of a wooden frame and covered with rich linen material in blue, purple, and scarlet.

Over this were waterproof coverings. Inside, the tabernacle was divided into two rooms. The smaller of these was called the "most holy place" or the "Holy of Holies." Only the high priest was

THE TABERNACLE

Holy of Holies   Ark of the Covenant

Table for loaves

Seven-branched lampstand

Incense altar

Laver – bronze ritual washing place for priests

Altar of burnt offering

Courtyard

Walls made from goat's hair

allowed into it and that was only once a year on the Day of Atonement. It was in this room that the Ark of the Covenant was kept.

In the other, larger room was a bronze altar on which incense was burned each morning and evening. There was also a seven-branched gold lampstand, called a menorah, and a gold table on which, once a week, 12 loaves of bread were placed, one for each of the 12 tribes of Israel.

Inside the tabernacle was the menorah, a seven-branched lampstand.

The tabernacle stood in a courtyard that was 54 yards (50 m) long and 27 yards (25 m) wide. Here, on a large altar, the priests burned animal sacrifices in their worship of God. Before the priests entered the tabernacle or offered a sacrifice, they washed their hands in a basin, called a laver.

Many years later, when the people of Israel were no longer traveling all the time, King David decided to build a temple in Jerusalem where the Ark of the Covenant could be kept and God

KING SOLOMON'S TEMPLE

Holy of Holies: only the high priest could enter here

Holy place

Store-rooms

Porch

Bronze washing bowl (laver)

Altar of sacrifice

could be worshiped. It was David's son, Solomon, who ordered the temple to be built, along the lines of the tabernacle. When it was finished, King Solomon led a grand service to dedicate the temple to God.

A second temple replaced Solomon's in 515 BCE, but the last Temple was built by King Herod the Great about 9 BCE. This was much bigger and grander than the previous ones. It was destroyed by the Romans in CE 70.

Herod's Temple had several extra courtyards in addition to the one for priests: these were the Court of Women – the nearest that women could

Solomon's greatest achievement as king of Israel was the building of the temple in Jerusalem.

go to the "Holy of Holies" – and the Court of the Gentiles – the nearest people who were not Jews (Gentiles) could go. Although there were prayers and sacrifices every day, the temple was

HEROD'S TEMPLE

Holy place

Holy of Holies: the high priest enters here only on the Day of Atonement

Inner court

Court of the Priests

Store-rooms

Altar

Court of Israel

Court of Women

especially full at religious festivals. Often Psalms were sung by people as they went to the temple.

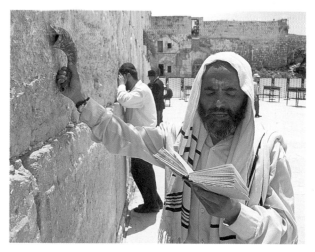

AT THE WESTERN WALL
This man is praying at the Western Wall. The *shophar*, or ram's horn, is blown at the start of a Jewish religious festival.

The Creation

I N THE BEGINNING God created heaven and earth. Water lay deep over the surface of the earth and the darkness was absolute. God said, "Let there be light." And suddenly there was light. And God saw that it was good. God divided the light, which was day, from the darkness, which was night. And so ended the first day and night of creation.

Next God said, "Let there be sky over the waters," and called the sky heaven; and this was on the second day.

On the third day the land rose up through the waters, and God called the dry land earth, and the waters sea. At once grasses took root on the earth and every kind of plant; buds opened, seeds sprouted, and trees grew heavy with fruit. And God saw that it was good.

On the fourth day God said, "There must be lights in the sky to divide night from day

On the first day God creates light

On the second day God creates sky

On the third day God creates land, sea, and every kind of plant

and to mark the seasons." For this God created two lights: the greater, which he called the sun, to shine over the day, and the smaller, the moon, to shine at night. Around the moon God set the stars. On the fifth day God created all the creatures of the sea and sky. Birds flew through the air, while in the watery depths great fish swam silently.

On the sixth day God made all the animals, from the wild beasts of desert and jungle to cattle grazing in the fields. And God saw that it was good.

And God said: "I shall make people in my own image to rule over them." And so God created people, both male and female, in God's own likeness. And that was on the morning and the evening of the sixth day.

On the seventh day God rested, for the work was done, and all was well with the world.

On the fourth day God creates the sun, the moon, and the stars

On the fifth day God creates the creatures of the sea and sky

On the sixth day God creates animals and people

The Garden of Eden

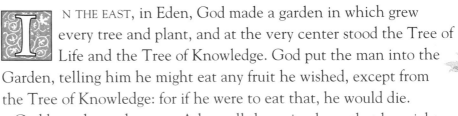

IN THE EAST, in Eden, God made a garden in which grew every tree and plant, and at the very center stood the Tree of Life and the Tree of Knowledge. God put the man into the Garden, telling him he might eat any fruit he wished, except from the Tree of Knowledge: for if he were to eat that, he would die.

God brought to the man, Adam, all the animals, so that he might name them. God then sent Adam into a deep sleep, and while he slept, took one of his ribs and out of it made a woman, so that Adam would have a wife. Both Adam and Eve, his wife, walked naked and happy in the Garden, and had no need of clothes.

Now the serpent, the most devious of all living creatures, questioned Eve, asking her if she could eat any fruit she pleased. "Yes," she said. "Any fruit except that from the Tree of Knowledge. If we eat that, we die."

"But you will not die," said the serpent. "Instead you will discover the difference between good and evil, and so will be equal with God."

The woman gazed at the Tree, and was tempted by the juicy fruit that would make her wise. She picked one and ate it; gave one to her husband, and he ate it. As they looked at each other, they

SERPENT
Serpents, or snakes, such as the Egyptian cobra above, were thought by many people to represent evil or Satan. Satan opposes God and tries to upset God's plans.

CHERUBIM
Cherubim were often represented as winged sphinxes, or human-headed lions, as in this Assyrian ivory carving. In the book of Genesis, cherubim act as God's attendants. They guard the Tree of Life, which is the symbol of eternal life.

Adam and Eve are happy in the Garden of Eden

Eve picks fruit from the Tree of Knowledge and gives one to Adam

became aware of their nakedness. They quickly gathered some fig leaves, which they sewed together to cover themselves.

In the cool of the evening they heard the voice of the Lord as God walked in the Garden, and they hid so that God would not see them.

God called to Adam, "Adam, where are you?"

Adam said, "I heard your voice, and I was afraid so I hid."

"If you are afraid then I know you must have eaten from the Tree whose fruit I told you not to eat."

"It was the woman who gave me the fruit."

And Eve said, "It was the serpent who tempted and deceived me."

Then God cursed the serpent, and banished him from the Garden. He gave clothes to Adam and Eve, saying, "Now that you know both good and evil, you must leave Eden. You cannot stay for fear you might eat also from the Tree of Life, and if you did that you would live forever." And God drove them out of the Garden, and into the world. At the east of Eden he stationed cherubim and placed a flaming sword to guard the entrance to the Garden and to the Tree of Life.

God drives Adam and Eve out of the Garden into the world

Cain and Abel

wheat
lentils
almonds
pistachio nuts
olives
figs
grapes

Cain works in the fields

Abel is a shepherd

CAIN'S OFFERING
God rejected Cain's offering for he did not give the best of his produce. Cain would have grown crops, such as the ones shown above.

E VE GAVE BIRTH TO TWO SONS. Abel, the younger, was a shepherd, while his brother, Cain, worked in the fields. There came a time when they both made offerings to God: Cain from his crops, Abel from the finest and fattest of his flock. God was well pleased with Abel's offering, but not with Cain's. This made Cain very angry, and his face darkened with rage.

Abel offers the finest of his flock to God, while Cain offers fruit and grain

Abel's offering
Cain's offering

Cain kills Abel because God preferred his offering

"Why are you angry?" the Lord God asked him. "You will succeed if you work hard; and if you do not, the sin will be yours."

But Cain was not soothed by these words. He followed his brother into the fields, and there attacked and murdered him.

"Cain, where is your brother?" asked the Lord.

"I do not know," Cain replied. "Am I my brother's keeper?"

But God knew what had happened. "Cain, what have you done? I see your brother's blood staining the earth. Now you are cursed, cursed to wander the world, an outcast from man and God."

"This punishment is greater than I can bear!" cried Cain in agony. "You, my God, are going to turn your face away from me and condemn me to wander the world, to be killed by anyone who passes me on the road."

But the Lord reassured him. "The man who kills Cain will bring upon himself a terrible punishment." And God made a mark on Cain so that everyone would recognize him, and when they saw the mark would know they must leave him unharmed.

With a heavy heart Cain departed, and went to live in the land of Nod, which lies to the east of Eden.

ABEL THE SHEPHERD
Abel would have spent all day leading his flock of sheep to good pastures, and keeping them from harm. Sheep provided meat, milk, wool, and skins. The fattest, most perfect lambs were always offered to God.

God puts a mark on Cain and condemns him to wander the world

mark of Cain

Noah's Ark

CYPRESS TREES
Cypress trees are found throughout the Bible lands. The wood is light, but strong and long-lasting. It was an ideal choice of timber for a boat as large as the ark.

AS THE YEARS PASSED, the descendants of Adam grew in number and spread to the four corners of the earth. But as they grew in number, so they grew in wickedness; and God, seeing violence and corruption everywhere, decided to destroy all the people and animals that had been created.

There was, however, one man whom the Lord loved, a good man who led an honest and hard-working life. His name was Noah, and God chose to save him, and to save also Noah's wife, and his three sons, Shem, Ham, and Japheth, and their wives.

"The world has grown wicked," God told Noah, "and I intend to destroy every living thing that I have made. But you, Noah, you and your family shall be saved.

Noah and his sons build the ark

Noah

"BUT WITH THEE WILL I ESTABLISH MY COVENANT; AND THOU SHALT COME INTO THE ARK, THOU, AND THY SONS, AND THY WIFE, AND THY SONS' WIVES WITH THEE."
GENESIS 6:18

"I shall cause a flood to rise over the land, and you must build an ark out of cypress wood that will float on the waters; it must be roofed with reeds and coated inside and out with tar. It must measure three-hundred cubits long, fifty cubits wide and thirty cubits high. It shall have three stories, with a door and a window in the side. In it you must make room for yourself and your family, and two – one male, one female – of every kind of creature, every kind of beast, reptile, and bird. And you must fill it with enough food for them and for yourselves. For it will rain for forty days and forty nights,

THERE WENT IN TWO AND TWO UNTO NOAH INTO THE ARK, THE MALE AND THE FEMALE, AS GOD HAD COMMANDED NOAH.
GENESIS: 7:9

The animals enter the ark, two by two

and life on earth will be extinct."

Noah did exactly as God had told him: he and his sons built the ark, making it watertight and stocking it with plenty of food of every variety for man and beast. When everything was ready, they led all the animals into the ark. Then they themselves went inside and God shut fast the door.

The skies darkened and it began to rain.

BOAT BUILDING
Noah and his sons would have built the ark by hand. The planks of wood were coated with tar to make the boat watertight. This traditional method of boat building is still practiced in parts of the Middle East today.

The Flood

THE RAIN CONTINUED for forty days and nights. The flood waters rose, lifting the ark up with them until it was floating as high as the hills. Finally even the mountain ranges were submerged, and everything that was alive perished: there was no living thing left on Earth.

But God had not forgotten Noah, and all who were with him on the ark. After a time the rains stopped. The days went by, and then a great wind blew up; and after the wind a calm, and slowly the waters began to go down. Eventually the ark came to rest on a mountain peak in Ararat.

THE DELUGE
This engraving by Gustave Doré captures the plight of people caught in the flood.

Every living thing perishes in the flood

AND THE WATERS PREVAILED, AND WERE INCREASED GREATLY UPON THE EARTH; AND THE ARK WENT UPON THE FACE OF THE WATERS.
GENESIS 7:18

Time passed, and Noah wanted to find out if the waters had subsided. Opening a window, he released a raven into the air to see if the bird would find anywhere to land. But the raven flew far and wide in every direction and saw nothing but water.

Next Noah released from the ark a dove; but she, too, flew in every direction without finding anywhere to land, for the waters still covered the earth. She returned to the ark, and Noah tenderly took her in. After seven days he again sent out the dove, and this time she came back in the evening with the leaf of an olive tree in her beak.

Noah knew by this that the waters were receding, and after waiting another seven days he sent out the dove once more. This time she did not return. Opening a window in the ark, Noah looked out and saw that the ground was dry.

God then spoke to Noah. "Now you must leave the ark, you, your wife, and your sons and their wives, and all the creatures you have with you. The world is for you and your children to govern, and the beasts on land and birds of the air and fish in the sea shall provide your food."

Then Noah built an altar in thanksgiving and made an offering on it to God. God was pleased with the sacrifice and blessed Noah and his family, telling them that they and their descendants would cover the earth.

As God spoke this blessing, a rainbow appeared in the sky. "This rainbow," God said, "is a sign that never again will the world be destroyed by flood; and in times to come when I cloud the sky with rain, afterward you will see a rainbow, and you will remember my promise, a promise made to you and to every living creature in the world."

ON DRY LAND
The mountainous area of Ararat in Turkey includes Mount Ararat where the ark is thought to have rested. Some people believe that Noah's ark still lies on this peak and expeditions have been sent to find its remains.

AND THE DOVE CAME IN TO NOAH IN THE EVENING; AND, LO, IN HER MOUTH WAS AN OLIVE LEAF.
GENESIS 8:11

The flood waters rise for forty days and nights

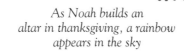

As Noah builds an altar in thanksgiving, a rainbow appears in the sky

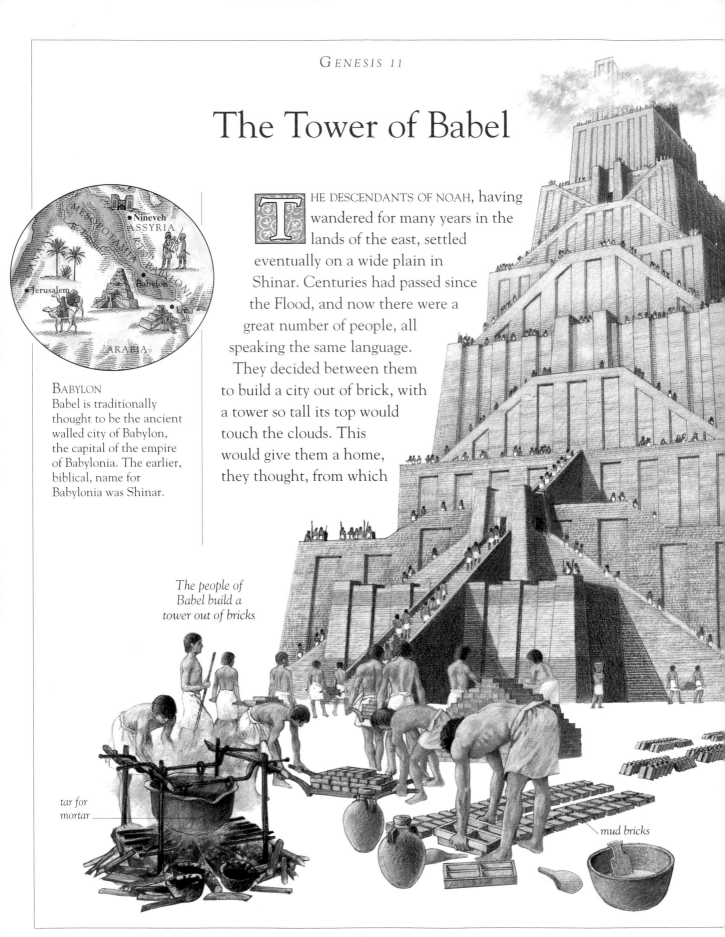

The Tower of Babel

THE DESCENDANTS OF NOAH, having wandered for many years in the lands of the east, settled eventually on a wide plain in Shinar. Centuries had passed since the Flood, and now there were a great number of people, all speaking the same language. They decided between them to build a city out of brick, with a tower so tall its top would touch the clouds. This would give them a home, they thought, from which

BABYLON
Babel is traditionally thought to be the ancient walled city of Babylon, the capital of the empire of Babylonia. The earlier, biblical, name for Babylonia was Shinar.

The people of Babel build a tower out of bricks

tar for mortar

mud bricks

no one could drive them out. More important, it would make them envied throughout the world.

And so they began to build, baking the bricks hard and using tar for mortar.

The Lord looked at the city that was taking shape, at the streets and the houses and the tower already rising up into the sky, and God said, "These people are growing vain. Soon there will be no limit to what they will want. I will confuse their speech, change the very words in their mouths, so that no one will understand what is said."

And so it was: soon everyone found that the words spoken by one person meant nothing to their neighbor.

This caused complete confusion. The building of the city, which was now called Babel because of the babble of voices within it, came to a stop. The people left the plain of Shinar and were scattered all over the world. And in every part of the world from that time on both men and women spoke in different languages.

ZIGGURAT
The tower of Babel may have been a ziggurat, or temple tower. Ziggurats have been found in Babylon and Ur. The pyramidlike buildings have outside staircases that lead to a temple at the top. Here, people believed they could be closer to the gods.

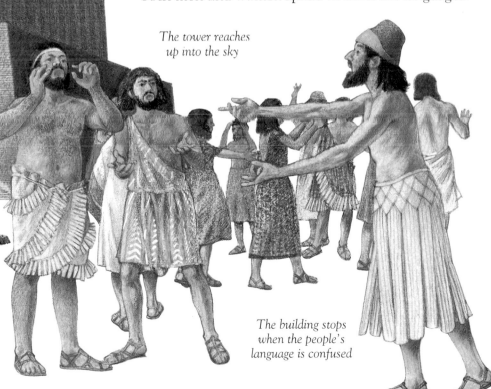

The tower reaches up into the sky

The building stops when the people's language is confused

MUD BRICKS
The tower of Babel would have been built out of mud bricks. This method of building is still used in parts of the Middle East today. Mud and straw are mixed together, shaped in wooden molds, then left to dry in the sun.

The Patriarchs

THE FIRST GREAT BIBLICAL leader of the people of Israel was Abraham. When he died, the leadership passed to his son, Isaac, and then in turn to Isaac's son, Jacob. These men are called the Patriarchs, which means male leaders or "fathers" of a family or tribe. The 12 sons of Jacob, including Joseph, were also considered Patriarchs, or founding fathers of Israel. They lived more than 1,500 years before Jesus.

During Abraham's life a special trust grew between his family and God. It began when the family left the great city of Ur and, together with their servants and animals, traveled first to Haran and then to the land of Canaan. When he left Haran, Abraham had no idea what sort of life awaited them. However, he believed that God wanted him to go to Canaan, so he set off on the long journey with his family. Because they trusted him, God made a covenant, or promise, with Abraham and his descendants: they would be his people and he would be their God.

God said to Abraham: "I will make nations of you and kings will come from you. I will give you the whole land of Canaan as an everlasting possession to you and your descendants. And I will be their God."

Although there were some towns in Canaan, the families of Abraham, Isaac, and Jacob moved from place to place, living in tents, finding areas where they could live without danger and where they had enough water and grazing for their sheep, goats, and other animals.

THE PATRIARCHS' FAMILY TREE

Abraham was the first of the Patriarchs. He was married to Sarah, but had a child (Ishmael) by Hagar, his wife's servant. Later, Sarah and Abraham had a son called Isaac.

Abraham's son, Isaac, married Rebekah. Her brother, Laban, was the father of Leah and Rachel who married Isaac's son Jacob.

Jacob was tricked into marrying Laban's eldest daughter Leah. Later he married her sister Rachel, whom he really loved.

Jacob had 12 sons and a daughter by his two wives and their servants, Zilpah and Bilhah. The 12 tribes of Israel were descended from his sons.

Sarah m. Abraham   Hagar

Isaac m. Rebekah   Laban   Ishmael

Esau   Jacob m. Leah and Rachel   Zilpah   Bilhah

Reuben   Simeon   Levi   Judah   Issachar   Zebulun   Dinah   Joseph   Benjamin   Gad   Asher   Dan   Naphtali

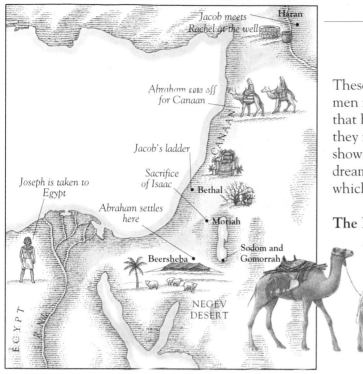

The map above shows the main events in the lives of the Patriarchs. Abraham and his people may have traveled across the desert to Canaan with camel caravans.

The God of Abraham, Isaac, and Jacob

Many important events happened to Abraham, Isaac, Jacob and other members of their family to test their faith in God and to give them greater understanding of God. For example, Abraham's obedience was shown when he was asked to sacrifice Isaac, his son. Later, when the time came for Isaac to be married, he learned to trust God through the way he met his wife, Rebekah. Years afterward, Jacob's faith in God became greater after he had a remarkable dream of a stairway stretching from Earth to Heaven.

These and other experiences helped the three men realize that God was involved in the things that happened to them in everyday life. Often they named places after something God had shown or taught them there. After Jacob had his dream, he decided to call the place "Bethal," which means "the house of God."

The Influence of the Patriarchs

Abraham, Isaac, and Jacob had great power, as did the heads of all families at that time. They were in charge of all family decisions, including the worship and sacrifices that were offered to God.

The Patriarch's word had to be obeyed and whenever he honored someone with a blessing, this could not be taken away. This is why Jacob, after he received a blessing from his father Isaac, became his heir, even though he had obtained the blessing by tricking his older brother, Esau.

The word "Israel" is first used in the Bible to refer to Jacob. One night Jacob wrestled with a stranger whom he thought was God. Afterward, God told Jacob that from then on he would be known as Israel, which means "the one who fights for God."

DESERT LIFE
Abraham and his people lived a nomadic life, moving from place to place. They probably lived on the outskirts of large towns, in tents similar to the Bedouin ones shown here.

Abram's Journey

ABRAM'S JOURNEY
The most likely route taken by Abram and Lot on their journey from Ur to Canaan. Lot finally settled in Sodom.

ABRAM WAS BORN in Ur in Mesopotamia. Now elderly, he had settled with his wife Sarai in Haran. It was a sadness for both of them that they had had no children. One day God spoke to Abram. "You must leave this place, Abram, and take your wife and your relations and servants and everything you possess, and move to the land that I will show you. Once there you will have my blessing, your name will be great, and your people will become a great nation."

Lot's people

Lot and Abram decide to part and Lot's people move to the plain of Jordan

Lot　　*Abram*

TREASURES FROM UR
This gold helmet and dagger with its decorative sheath were discovered in Ur, a powerful city-state and the birthplace of Abram and Lot.

So Abram, with his wife Sarai and his nephew Lot, with his servants, his gold and silver, his tents, his donkeys and camels, sheep, and cattle, traveled south toward the land of Canaan. But at the first place they settled there was not enough fertile land. Abram's shepherds began to fight Lot's shepherds for the best place to graze their flocks. Abram said to Lot, "Let us not quarrel. The whole country lies before us. If you go to the east, then I will go to the west, and there will be plenty for everyone."

So Abram and his people settled in Canaan, while Lot looked to the east and saw the plain of Jordan. It was as lush and green as a well-watered garden. And there Lot agreed to go, he and his people settling in Sodom, one of the cities of the plain, whose inhabitants were known to be great sinners.

The Lord spoke again to Abram. "Look around you: all this land will belong to you and to your many descendants."

"But how can I have descendants?" said Abram, "I am an old man and I have no children."

"You will have a son," God told him. "And your son will have children, and his children's children will be as many in number as there are stars in the sky."

THE LORD MADE A COVENANT WITH ABRAM SAYING, "UNTO THY SEED HAVE I GIVEN THIS LAND, FROM THE RIVER OF EGYPT UNTO THE GREAT RIVER, THE RIVER EUPHRATES."
GENESIS 15:18

Sarai

Abram's people settle in the land of Canaan

Then God told Abram to make a sacrifice: to take a cow, a she-goat, and a ram; to kill the animals, cut them in half, and lay them side by side; to kill also a turtledove and a young pigeon.

This Abram did, dividing the animals in two, and leaving the birds whole. Later in the day he beat off the birds of prey, which greedily swooped down upon the carcasses. As the sun set he fell into a deep sleep, and while he slept he was seized with a terrible fear. But then he heard the voice of God speaking to him. He promised Abram that all would be well, and that he and his descendants would one day live in prosperity and die in peace in this land.

Night fell; and suddenly there came out of the darkness smoke and flames and a burning torch, which passed over Abram's sacrifice.

DESERT WANDERINGS
Abram and his family led a nomadic life. They traveled from place to place, looking for grazing land and water for their animals. They carried all their possessions on camels, and lived in tents. The Bedouin people live a similar life in the desert today.

Abram, Sarai, and Hagar

TENT DWELLERS
Desert dwellers today, such as these modern Bedouin, live much like Abram's family did. Because they constantly travel with their flocks to new grazing land, all of their possessions must be light, and easy to roll up. Waterproof tents woven out of coarse goat hair are homes well-suited to this way of living.

SARAI WAS GROWING OLD and still she had no children. She went to her husband, Abram, and told him that he should have a child by Hagar, her servant. "Look on Hagar," she said, "as though she were your wife."

This Abram did, but once Hagar realized she was going to have a baby, she began to be conceited and act rudely toward her mistress. "Hagar now looks down on me and insults me," Sarai complained to Abram.

"You must deal with her as you think right," Abram replied.

Upon this Sarai began to treat her servant so harshly that Hagar ran away into the desert.

An angel found Hagar beside a spring in the wilderness, where she was weeping.

"What are you doing here?" he asked her.

"I am running away from my cruel mistress."

"You must return and behave well toward her. You are soon to give birth to

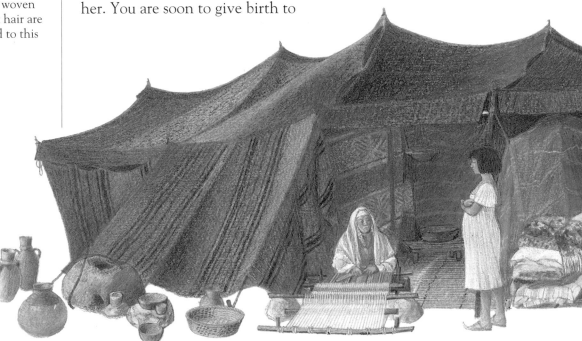

Hagar is expecting a child by Abram and begins to act rudely toward Sarai

Hagar runs into the wilderness and weeps, as Sarai has treated her harshly

a son whose name shall be Ishmael, and his descendants will be numbered in millions."

So Hagar returned and shortly afterward gave birth to a boy. Abram was then eighty-six years old. He looked at his son and gave him the name Ishmael, which means "God hears."

When Abram was ninety-nine, God appeared to him and said, "You shall be the father of many nations, and to mark this you must change your name to Abraham. I will keep my promise to you, and Canaan shall belong to you and your descendants forever; and I will be their God. Among your people every male must be circumcised now, and every male child of future generations. This will be a sign that you will keep your promise to me. From now on your wife must be called Sarah, and she will be the mother of your son."

Abraham laughed to himself at the idea that a man of one hundred and a woman of ninety should have a child. But God said, "Sarah will indeed have a son, and you shall call him Isaac, and he will be the father of princes. It will be with Isaac that my promise shall be continued, a covenant to be kept with all his descendants throughout all their generations.

"As for Ishmael, I will bless him and always look after him. He will lead a long and prosperous life, and will have many children. He will be a great power in the land, even though it is his brother, Isaac, whom I have chosen as the father of my people."

MOTHER AND CHILD
This Bedouin woman is holding her little child close to her. The Israelites considered children to be a gift from God. To be barren and unable to have a child, as Sarai was for many years, would have caused much heartache. Children spent most of their early years with their mothers.

Hagar   *Abram*

Hagar returns home and gives birth to a boy, and Abram calls him Ishmael

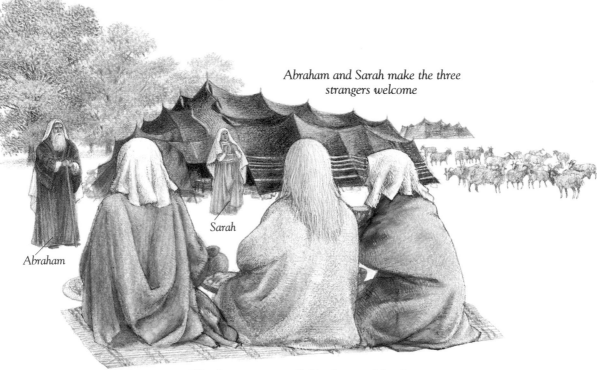

Abraham and Sarah make the three strangers welcome

Sarah

Abraham

The three strangers tell Abraham and Sarah that they will have a son

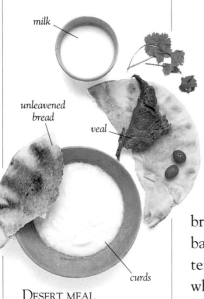

milk

unleavened bread

veal

curds

DESERT MEAL
Sarah may have prepared a meal of bread, probably unleavened (made without yeast); milk, from a goat or sheep; curds, made from soured milk; and veal. Serving meat and milk together was not prohibited to Jews until after Moses, so this was a gracious meal then.

Time passed, and God appeared to Abraham near the trees of Mamre in the heat of the day.

Abraham was sitting at the entrance to his tent when he looked up and saw three strangers standing before him. At once, he came out to greet them. "My lords," Abraham said, bowing low. "If I have found favor with you, do not pass me by. Come, sit under this tree so you may wash your feet and rest, then we will bring you food, for we are your servants." Abraham then hurried back into the tent, giving orders to Sarah to bake bread, and for a tender young calf to be roasted. He stood by them under the tree while they ate.

"Where is your wife?" they asked.

"She is in the tent."

"Soon she will bear you a son."

Now Sarah was listening to this and she laughed at the idea that such an old woman should bear a child. But God heard her and rebuked her.

"Do you think there is anything too difficult for God to do?" he asked her.

Sodom and Gomorrah

OD TOLD ABRAHAM that the cities of Sodom and Gomorrah would be destroyed, because their inhabitants were guilty of terrible crimes.

"If you find even ten righteous people," Abraham implored God, "will you have mercy and save these cities from destruction?"

"If I find ten good people," said the Lord, "I will not destroy them."

Two angels left for Sodom. They arrived there in the evening, where they were met at the city gates by Abraham's nephew, Lot. He welcomed them to his house, and spread before them a feast that he had prepared with his own hands.

No sooner had they finished eating than they heard the noise of a large crowd gathering. It was the men of Sodom: they were demanding that Lot hand over to them his two guests for their own pleasure.

Lot was full of anger and went out to speak to the crowd. "I would rather give you my daughters, to do with as you please," he said.

THE LORD SAID, "BECAUSE THE CRY OF SODOM AND GOMORRAH IS GREAT, AND BECAUSE THEIR SIN IS VERY GRIEVOUS, I WILL GO DOWN."
GENESIS 18:20-21

Lot goes out to speak to the crowd

Lot

A large crowd gathers threateningly outside Lot's home

37

"But these men you must not harm, for they are guests under my roof."

The crowd was in a frenzy and took no notice; the men only shouted louder and tried to force their way in. Suddenly Lot felt the angels' hands on his shoulders: they pulled him inside and shut the door.

Then they struck the crowd with blindness, so that the men could no longer see where they were.

The two angels said to Lot, "Are there any other members of your family here? You must go to them and tell them to leave at once, or they will die when the city is destroyed." Lot hurried to his daughters' husbands and warned them of what was about to happen, but they would not listen and refused to move. Then the angels told Lot that he himself must leave. "Take your wife and both your daughters, and go quickly, for we must destroy this place and all its wickedness."

By now dawn was breaking, and the angels urged Lot to be gone.

God rains down fire and brimstone on Sodom and Gomorrah

CITIES OF THE PLAIN
The cities of Sodom and Gomorrah probably lay in what is now the southern end of the Dead Sea. This area was once dry land that was very fertile. It is thought that an earthquake caused the Dead Sea to spread and cover the towns.

When they saw him hesitate, they took him by the hand and led him through the deserted streets and out beyond the city walls.

"Run as fast as you can, and make straight for the mountains. Do not look behind you, no matter what."

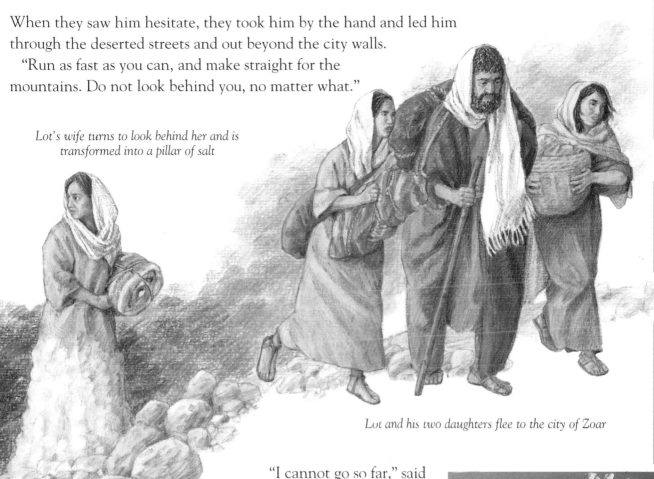

Lot's wife turns to look behind her and is transformed into a pillar of salt

Lot and his two daughters flee to the city of Zoar

"I cannot go so far," said Lot. "The mountains are too distant. Let me stay instead in the city of Zoar. Let me live there, and let it not be destroyed."

And to this the angels agreed.

By the time the sun had risen, Lot had reached Zoar. Then the Lord God rained down fire and burning stone on Sodom and Gomorrah, so that they and their people and the surrounding plain and everything that grew and moved upon it were utterly destroyed. Feeling the heat and hearing the noise, Lot's wife turned to look behind her. Instantly she was transformed into a pillar of salt.

The next morning Abraham rose early, and going to the place where he had talked with the Lord, he looked toward Sodom and Gomorrah. Instead of those two great cities of the plain he saw nothing but thick black smoke, like the smoke from a giant furnace.

PILLARS OF SALT
Because of the large amount of salt in the Dead Sea, nothing can live there – hence its name. There are clusters of salt in the water, serving as a reminder of the terrible fate of Lot's wife when she was turned into a pillar of salt.

Abraham's Two Sons

CIRCUMCISION
This painting by Fra Angelico shows Jesus being circumcised. In this ceremony the foreskin of a baby boy is removed. Many nations practiced circumcision, but for the Israelites it had a special meaning. It was a sign of the agreement, or covenant, between God and their people.

T HAPPENED just as the Lord had said. When Abraham was a hundred years old, Sarah gave birth to a son whom they named Isaac from the word "laugh"; and when the baby was eight days old, he was circumcised. Both parents were overjoyed that at last they had a child, and Abraham gave a magnificent feast in celebration.

"Who would have thought that I at my age would have given birth," Sarah exclaimed. "God made me laugh with

Isaac

Ishmael

Sarah has a son by Abraham called Isaac

Abraham sends Hagar and Ishmael into the desert of Beersheba

WATER SKIN
The water carrier that Abraham gave to Hagar would have looked like this Bedouin water skin.

happiness so that all who heard should rejoice with me."

Soon, however, Sarah noticed that Hagar's son, Ishmael, was making fun of Isaac. "Ishmael must go!" she insisted. "You must turn him out, and his mother with him!

Abraham was saddened for he loved both his sons, but God reassured him. "Do as Sarah asks, for I will look after both Ishmael and Isaac. They will both live to be the founders of great nations."

Early the next morning Abraham gave Hagar some bread and a

leather skin filled with water and sent her into the desert of Beersheba with Ishmael.

The two of them wandered many miles through the hot, stony wilderness. Soon the bread was eaten, the skin dry, and there was no water to be found anywhere. Believing that death was near, Hagar laid her child under a bush, and then, weeping, went to sit by herself some way off so that she would not see him die.

Suddenly she heard the voice of an angel. "Do not be afraid," said the voice. "God will not let Ishmael die, for he has a glorious future before him. Go to him now, and take him by the hand."

As Hagar dried her eyes, she saw in front of her a spring. Eagerly she filled her skin, then went to Ishmael and gave him the water to drink.

ISHMAEL
The Arab people are traditionally believed to be the descendants of Ishmael.

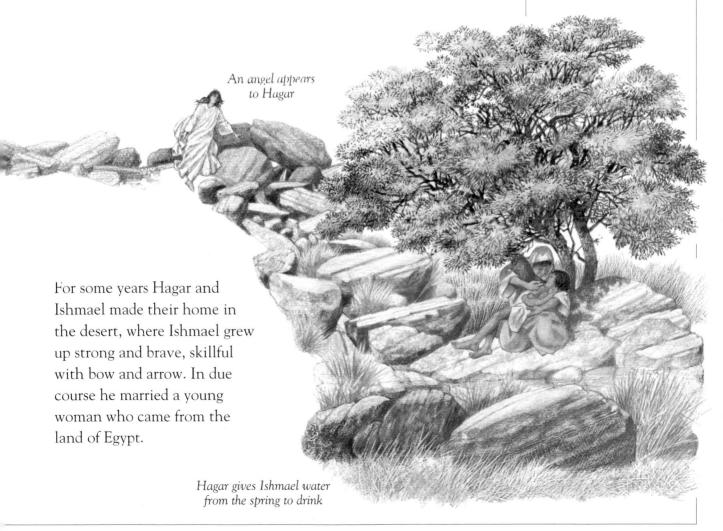

An angel appears to Hagar

For some years Hagar and Ishmael made their home in the desert, where Ishmael grew up strong and brave, skillful with bow and arrow. In due course he married a young woman who came from the land of Egypt.

Hagar gives Ishmael water from the spring to drink

The Sacrifice of Isaac

NEGEV DESERT
Abraham and Isaac set off from their home in Beersheba. They journeyed through the Negev Desert, in southern Canaan, for three days until they reached Moriah.

GOD SPOKE TO ABRAHAM, in order to test his faith. "With your beloved son Isaac you must go to the land of Moriah, to a certain mountain which I will show you. There, instead of a goat or lamb, you must sacrifice your son on the fire."

The next morning, obedient to God's will, Abraham saddled a donkey, and set off for Moriah, taking Isaac and two servants with him. When they got to the mountains, Abraham stopped to cut some wood, giving it to his son to carry. He himself took a sharp knife and a flaming torch with which to light the fire. "You must stay here with the donkey," he told the two men. "We are going up the mountain to pray and make an offering to God."

"Father," said Isaac as they started on their way. "We have the wood for a fire, but where is the lamb to be sacrificed?"

"God will provide," answered Abraham.

When they reached the place chosen by God, Abraham built an altar on which he piled the wood; then, tying Isaac's arms tightly to his sides, he placed the boy on top of the pile. Abraham lifted the knife high above his head, preparing to plunge it into Isaac's breast. But at that moment he heard the voice of the angel of the Lord.

DOME OF THE ROCK
The mosque in Jerusalem is built on a rock, thought by many to be Mount Moriah, where Abraham was going to sacrifice Isaac. It is also the site of Solomon's Temple and Herod's Temple.

The two servants wait with the donkey

Abraham and Isaac go up the mountain to offer a sacrifice to God

"Abraham, Abraham, do not hurt your son. You have proved your perfect love of God by your willingness to sacrifice even your child."

The angel of the Lord tells Abraham not to hurt Isaac

RAMS IN THE THICKET
Abraham saw a ram, or male sheep, caught in a bush and sacrificed it instead of his son. The ram's horns may have become entangled as it tried to feed from the branches of the bush.

A ram caught in a thicket is sacrificed instead of Isaac

Looking around, Abraham saw a ram caught by the horns in the tangled branches of a bush. He untied Isaac, and seizing hold of the ram, put the animal on the altar in place of his son.

The angel spoke again. "Because you have done this for the love of God, you will be blessed, and your son, and your son's sons will be blessed; and they shall be as many in number as the stars in the sky."

Then Abraham and Isaac together came down from the mountain, and with the two servants returned to Beersheba.

"IN BLESSING I WILL BLESS THEE, AND IN MULTIPLYING I WILL MULTIPLY THY SEED AS THE STARS OF THE HEAVEN, AND AS THE SAND WHICH IS UPON THE SEASHORE."
GENESIS 22:17

Isaac and Rebekah

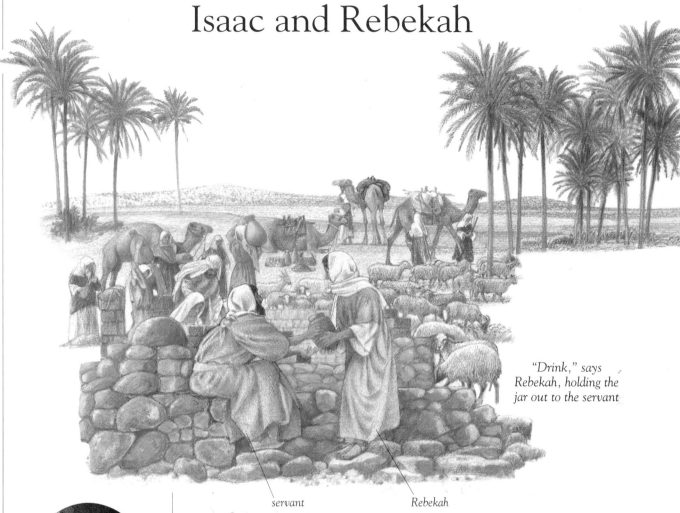

"Drink," says Rebekah, holding the jar out to the servant

servant   Rebekah

WATER CARRIER
Women like Rebekah often went to fetch water from a community well or cistern. These usually lay outside the city gates.

SARAH WAS DEAD, and Abraham knew he himself had not long to live. He sent for his most trusted servant. "My people are settled in Canaan, but I do not want my son to marry a Canaanite. You must go to the land of my birth, and from there bring back a wife for Isaac."

And so the servant set off for the city of Nahor in Mesopotamia, taking with him a train of ten camels laden with rich gifts. He arrived outside the city walls in the evening when the women were gathering to draw water at the well. As he watched them, he prayed to God for a sign: "Let her whom I ask for water be the wife for Isaac."

Almost before he had finished his prayer, a young girl carrying a water jar came to take her turn at the well. Her name was Rebekah, and she was very beautiful. The servant went up to her. "Will you let me drink from your jar?" he asked.

"Drink," she said, holding the jar out to him. "And now I will fetch water for your camels as well."

The servant was overjoyed at her kindness.

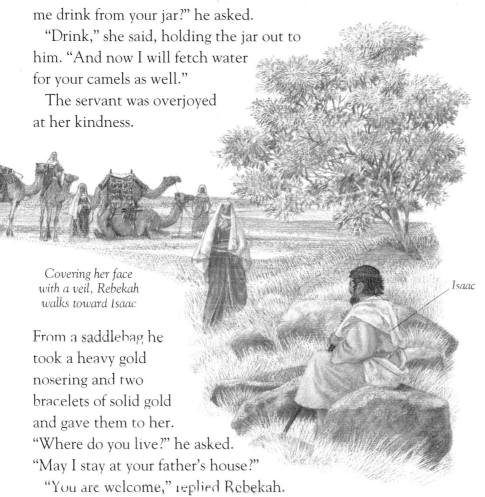

Covering her face with a veil, Rebekah walks toward Isaac

Isaac

From a saddlebag he took a heavy gold nosering and two bracelets of solid gold and gave them to her. "Where do you live?" he asked. "May I stay at your father's house?"

"You are welcome," replied Rebekah. Then she hurried home to tell her family. Her brother Laban welcomed the stranger, soon recognizing that it was God's will that Rebekah should return with him to Canaan.

Abraham's servant, having sent a prayer of thanks to God, made gifts to Rebekah of gold and silver jewelry and beautiful embroidered cloth. The next morning Rebekah said good-bye to her family, then set off with her nurse and servants for her new home.

Isaac was praying in the fields at twilight when he saw the camel caravan approaching through the dusk.

Covering her face with a veil, Rebekah dismounted. The servant described everything that had happened, and Isaac took Rebekah by the hand and led her to his tent.

Soon afterward they were married, and Isaac loved his wife and was comforted by her for the death of his mother, Sarah.

CAMEL
Abraham's large herd of camels was a sign of his family's wealth. The camel was used as a working animal. It was capable of carrying up to 400 lbs (180 kg) and could travel across the desert at about 8 to 10 miles (13 to 16 km) an hour.

NOSERING
The nosering given to Rebekah may have looked like the one this Bedouin woman is wearing. Mesopotamian women often wore jewelry, including rings, necklaces, and bracelets.

Esau and Jacob

IBEX
Esau would have hunted game, such as the ibex, a type of wild goat, whose meat was highly prized. Ibex are still found in rocky areas of the Middle East today.

AFTER MANY YEARS of childlessness Rebekah gave birth to twin boys. The elder, who was covered from head to toe with thick red hair, they named Esau. The younger, born holding his twin's heel, they called Jacob. Esau, whom Isaac loved best, grew up a strong and adventurous hunter, while Jacob, his mother's favorite, preferred staying at home.

One day Jacob was cooking some lentil stew when his brother came in, faint with hunger. "Quick, I'm famished! Give me some of that!" Esau demanded.

"I will," Jacob replied, "if you give up your rights as firstborn to me."

Esau laughed. "What use to me are rights when what I want is a good meal!"

"Then give me your word." And Esau gave his word, and so exchanged his birthright for a plateful of stew and some bread.

Isaac, old and blind and near to death, asked Esau to shoot a deer and prepare the dish of venison he so loved. "I want to taste it one last time so that I may bless you before I die," he told him.

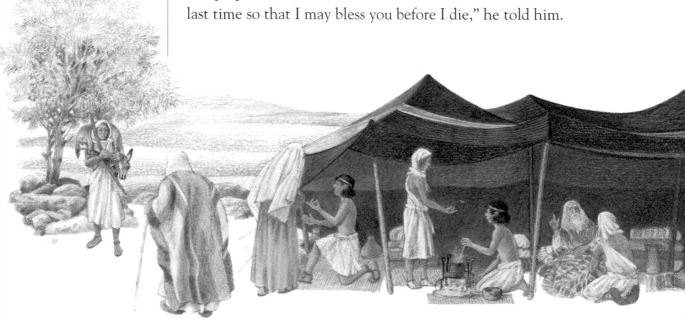

Esau, whom Isaac loves best, is a hunter

Jacob, Rebekah's favorite, prefers staying at home

Esau exchanges his birthright for a plateful of stew

Rebekah overheard these words and determined that Jacob, not Esau, should receive his father's blessing. "I will cook the dish," she said, "and you must take it to your father in Esau's place. Go now and fetch me two young goats."

"But he will know I am not Esau!" said Jacob. "Esau is covered in hair, and my skin is smooth. He will know that I am deceiving him, and will put a curse on me!"

"Do as I say, and all will be well." And Rebekah dressed Jacob in his brother's clothes and covered his hands and shoulders with goatskin. She gave him some bread and a bowl of stew made from goat's meat. Then she sent him to his father.

"Who are you?" Isaac asked, puzzled. "Come near me so that I may feel you. The voice is Jacob's voice, but the hands are the hands of Esau. Are you really my eldest son?"

"I am," Jacob lied.

So Isaac was deceived. Believing that it was Esau who was with him, he ate the food that had been brought to him. He blessed Jacob and promised that he should have everything due to the firstborn. "May you be happy and prosperous, and may good fortune come to all who wish you well."

LENTIL STEW
Esau sold his birthright to Jacob in exchange for a "mess of portage," or red lentil stew, which he scooped up with thin, unleavened bread. This was a common meal in Old Testament times.

Rebekah discovers that Isaac is to give Esau his blessing

Rebekah helps Jacob to disguise himself as Esau

Isaac blesses Jacob instead of Esau, while Rebekah looks on

Scarcely had Jacob left his father's tent than Esau arrived home from the hunt. Expertly he prepared the dish of venison and took it to Isaac. "Here is your favorite dish, father," he said.

"Who are you?" asked the old man.

"I am Esau, your eldest son."

"Then who is it who has just now been with me, and to whom I have given my blessing?" Isaac asked, his voice trembling.

When Esau heard his father's words, he cried out bitterly. He realized the trick that had been played, and he begged his father to bless him and give him his rights.

"I will bless you," said Isaac, "but I cannot give you what I have already promised to your brother." Isaac knew that the blessing was given before God, and it could not be altered.

Esau was filled with hatred for Jacob. He knew that Isaac would soon be dead, so he planned to kill Jacob as soon as the period of mourning for his father's death had passed. But Rebekah heard of his plot and was able to warn Jacob. "Your brother is planning to kill you," she told him. "Go at once to my brother Laban in Haran, and stay there until Esau's anger cools. I will let you know when it is safe to return." So Jacob left Beersheba and set out for Haran.

JACOB'S JOURNEY
Jacob set off from Beersheba in southern Canaan. He stopped at Bethel, where God appeared to him in a dream. From there he may have followed the route of the trade caravans and passed through major cities, such as Damascus, before reaching Haran.

Esau cries out when he realizes that Isaac has blessed Jacob

Rebekah tells Jacob to leave for Haran, to escape his brother's anger

Jacob's Ladder

O N HIS WAY TO STAY with Laban, Jacob stopped for the night. He picked up a large, smooth stone to use as a pillow and lay down to sleep.

He dreamed he saw a stairway reaching up to heaven, with angels moving up and down it. At the top of the stairway was God. "I am the God of Abraham and of your father Isaac," said the Lord to Jacob. "And I will give the land on which you lie to you and your descendants."

When Jacob awoke early the next morning, he was struck with wonder. "This is a holy place, for God was here and I did not know it." He took the stone which he had used as a pillow, and having stood it upright, poured oil over it. Then he named the place "Bethel," meaning the house of God.

He dreams of a stairway reaching like a ladder to heaven

Jacob falls asleep, using a stone as a pillow

AND HE DREAMED, AND BEHOLD A LADDER SET UP ON THE EARTH, AND THE TOP OF IT REACHED TO HEAVEN: AND BEHOLD THE ANGELS OF GOD ASCENDING AND DESCENDING ON IT.
GENESIS 28:12

Jacob and Rachel

Jacob watches as Rachel approaches the well

SHEPHERDESS
Rachel was a shepherdess. She would have tended her flock with care, protecting it from harm.

ACOB CONTINUED on his journey from Bethel. Eventually he came near Haran, in northern Mesopotamia. He saw a field in the middle of which was a well covered by a heavy stone. Around the well lay several flocks of sheep, being tended by shepherds. Every day when it was time for the sheep to drink, the shepherds would lift off the stone and draw water for the sheep from the well. They would then replace the stone over the mouth of the well.

Jacob greeted the shepherds. "Can you tell me the name of this place?" he asked.

"You are in Haran," they told him.

"Do you know Laban?"

"We know him well," they replied. "His daughter, Rachel, will be coming soon to draw water for their sheep."

Jacob sat down and waited, and then he saw Rachel approaching, driving before her a flock of sheep. Jacob thought she was very beautiful.

As she drew near, Jacob lifted the stone from the top of the well and helped her water her father's sheep. "I am Jacob, the son of Isaac. My mother is Rebekah, your father's sister," he told Rachel. Then he embraced and kissed her.

Rachel was delighted to see her cousin. She ran at once to tell her father the news.

Laban, too, was filled with joy, and hurried to meet his nephew.

JACOB'S KISS
On first meeting Rachel, Jacob kisses her. This painting by William Dyce captures the moment.

On hearing from Rachel that Jacob is here, Laban comes out to greet his nephew

Rachel and Leah wait to welcome Jacob

Throwing his arms around Jacob, he told him how glad he was that he had come. "You are welcome in my house," he said. "You, my sister's son, must come and stay with me."

They went back to his home where both Rachel and her elder sister, Leah, were waiting to welcome Jacob to their father's house.

So Jacob, having told his uncle all that had happened between himself and Esau, stayed with Laban for a month. During that time he worked hard, doing willingly whatever Laban asked him.

HEBREW BEAUTY
Rachel would have been young, with a natural beauty like this girl.

Jacob's Wedding

AND JACOB SERVED SEVEN
YEARS FOR RACHEL; AND THEY
SEEMED UNTO HIM BUT A FEW
DAYS, FOR THE LOVE HE
HAD TO HER.
GENESIS 29:20

WHEN JACOB HAD BEEN WORKING for his uncle for a month, Laban said to him, "It is not right that you should work for nothing. Tell me what I should give you in payment."

Now Jacob looked at Laban's two daughters, Rachel and Leah. Leah was plain, but Rachel was slender and beautiful, and it was she whom Jacob loved.

Laban

Laban gives a feast to celebrate the marriage of his daughter

VEILED SECRET
On her wedding day, Leah would have worn a veil over her face, like the one this Bedouin woman is wearing. This explains how Jacob was tricked into believing that Leah was Rachel.

"I will work for nothing," he said to Laban, "if at the end of seven years you will give me Rachel as my wife."

"I would rather she marry you than anyone," said Laban. "At the end of that time she shall be yours."

So for seven years Jacob worked as hard as he knew how. He loved Rachel so much and was so happy in her presence that the time passed quickly, each year seeming no more than a week in length.

At the end of seven years, Jacob went to Laban to claim his reward. "Now let me marry Rachel, as you promised."

Laban called together all his friends and family, and gave a great feast to celebrate the marriage of his daughter. But that night, when it was dark, he sent Leah to Jacob in Rachel's place. In the morning, when Jacob saw the older, not the younger, sister lying by his side, he realized he had been tricked. "How could you do this?" he asked Laban angrily. "Did we not make a bargain? Have I not worked for you for seven years so that I might have Rachel as my wife?"

Laban shrugged. "In this country it is the custom for the elder daughter to marry first. Leah is the elder, so it is right that you should take her for your wife." He laid a hand soothingly on Jacob's arm. "However," he continued, "finish the wedding week's festivities. Then you may marry Rachel as well if you will work for me for another seven years."

To this Jacob agreed; a week later Rachel became his wife and for seven more years Jacob worked for Laban.

WEDDING FEAST
The Bible says that the wedding feast of Jacob and Leah lasted for one week. During this time family and friends would have gathered to sing, dance, and play music, as in this modern-day village wedding in Iran.

Jacob is angry with Laban for tricking him into marrying Leah

Laban   Jacob

Leah

Jacob marries Rachel a week after Leah

Of his two wives, Jacob loved Rachel best. But while Rachel remained childless, Leah bore her husband six sons and a daughter. Rachel grew envious of her sister, and in her unhappiness turned against Jacob. " Why do you not give me children?" she demanded.

"I am not God," Jacob coldly answered her.

But in time Rachel, too, conceived, giving birth to a boy, called Joseph. Once she had her baby, Rachel's sadness disappeared.

While Leah has many children, Rachel remains childless

Leah   Rachel

53

Jacob's Return

Jacob and his family journey home to Canaan

stranger

Jacob

A stranger wrestles with Jacob

JABBOK RIVER
Jacob sent his family across the Jabbok River, so that he could spend some time alone. The fast-flowing Jabbok feeds into the River Jordan.

AFTER THE BIRTH OF JOSEPH, Jacob decided it was time to leave Laban, who was becoming jealous of his skills as a shepherd and his growing wealth. He sent a message to Esau to say he was on his way home and that he hoped Esau would look favorably on him. And then, taking with him his wives and children, all his servants, his herds and flocks, he started out for Canaan. Almost at once word came that Esau was coming to meet him with a force of four hundred men.

"I fear from this that he means to attack," said Jacob, and prayed to God to save him. He divided his own company into two parts, so that if Esau did attack at least half would escape. Then he chose a large number of cattle, camels, and donkeys to give to his brother.

That evening Jacob sent all the men, women, and children, together with his possessions, across the Jabbok River so that he might have some time alone.

Suddenly, and from nowhere, a stranger appeared and began to wrestle with him. All night they fought in silence.

ESAU MEETS JACOB
The dramatic reunion of the two brothers is realistically captured by Gustave Doré in this 19th-century engraving.

Jacob   Esau

Jacob and Esau are reunited

At dawn the stranger said, "It is now morning, and I must leave. Tell me, what is your name?"

" My name is Jacob."

"You shall not be called Jacob any longer, but Israel, for you have struggled with God and with men, and you have prevailed." And with that the stranger was gone. As the sun rose and light returned to the fields, Jacob realized that he had come face to face with God.

He had hardly caught up with his people when they saw a cloud of dust on the road, signaling the approach of Esau and his four hundred men. Jacob hurried forward, then bowed down before his brother. Esau threw his arms around him and kissed him, and they both wept. "Welcome, brother," Esau said. "You and yours are welcome home."

JACOB BOWED HIMSELF TO THE GROUND SEVEN TIMES, UNTIL HE CAME NEAR TO HIS BROTHER. ESAU RAN TO MEET HIM, AND EMBRACED HIM, AND FELL ON HIS NECK, AND KISSED HIM: AND THEY WEPT.
GENESIS 33:3-4

Joseph's Dreams

saffron

cochineal

pomegranate

mollusk shell

kermes insect

NATURAL DYES
Joseph's coat could have been dyed with colors similar to those shown above. Orange came from the saffron flower, pink from the cochineal insect, blue from the rind of a pomegranate, purple from the mollusk shell, and red from the kermes insect.

ACOB LIVED IN CANAAN with his twelve sons. Of all his sons, he loved Joseph the most, as his mother was his beloved wife Rachel. He made Joseph a beautiful coat woven in all the brilliant colors of the rainbow. Jacob's other sons were jealous of Joseph because he was so favored, and when they saw him in his coat of many colors they hated him. One night Joseph had a dream, and when he had told his brothers his dream, they hated him even more.

"I dreamed," he said, "that we were in the fields at harvest, tying up sheaves of wheat. My sheaf of wheat stood upright, while your sheaves bowed down to it."

Soon afterward Joseph had another dream. "I dreamed," he said, "that the sun and moon in the sky and eleven stars were all bowing down to me."

When the brothers heard his words they were furious. A few days later they took their flocks to graze in fields some distance away. Jacob sent Joseph to see that all was well. The brothers had a clear view

Joseph tells his brothers his dreams

Jacob gives Joseph a beautiful coat

of the road and saw Joseph approaching in his multicolored coat. "Now is our chance – we could kill him and throw him into this pit. We can say that a wild animal attacked him."

But Reuben, who had a kind heart, spoke out. "Don't let us kill him: we don't want his blood on our hands. Much better just to throw him into the pit and leave him to his fate." And to this the brothers agreed – not knowing that secretly Reuben was planning to return later, rescue Joseph, and take him home.

When Joseph reached them, his brothers attacked him at once, ripping off his coat and throwing him into the pit. They left him there without food or water. Then they sat down to eat.

At twilight a group of Ishmaelites came by. They were on their way to Egypt with camels loaded with spices, balm, and myrrh. Judah suggested that they sell Joseph as a slave to the travelers. Then they would be rid of the brother they hated without having to kill him.

So Joseph was sold for twenty pieces of silver. And the Ishmaelites took him with them into Egypt.

Meanwhile the brothers killed a young kid and dipped Joseph's coat in its blood. Their father was filled with horror when they showed it to him. "This is Joseph's coat! My beloved son must have been killed by some wild beast!" Jacob tore his clothes in grief and wept, and no one was able to comfort him.

balm
cinnamon
fennel seeds
black peppercorns
myrrh oil
myrrh resin

ISHMAELITE GOODS
The Ishmaelite traders carried goods such as these from Arabia to Egypt. Cinnamon was used as a spice and a perfume, balm and fennel were used in medicine, myrrh resin and oil for anointing and embalming bodies.

A group of Ishmaelite traders are on their way to Egypt

The brothers throw Joseph into the pit

The brothers sell Joseph to the Ishmaelites

Joseph's coat

Joseph the Slave

AND SHE CAUGHT HIM BY HIS GARMENT, SAYING, "LIE WITH ME," AND HE LEFT HIS GARMENT IN HER HAND, AND FLED.
GENESIS 39:12

WHEN THE ISHMAELITES ARRIVED IN EGYPT THEY sold Joseph to one of Pharaoh's officers, Potiphar, captain of the guard. Joseph worked hard for Potiphar, who was so impressed by his skills that he made him head of his household.

Now Joseph was a handsome young man, and before long he

The Ishmaelites sell Joseph to Potiphar

Joseph

Potiphar

Potiphar's wife tries to seduce Joseph

WOMEN IN EGYPT
This Egyptian wall painting shows an official being offered food by his wife. Egyptian women, such as Potiphar's wife, could own and manage property.

caught the eye of Potiphar's wife. She tried very hard to seduce him, but Joseph resisted her. "Your husband trusts me," he said. "You cannot ask me to betray him." Potiphar's wife did not care for her husband or for Joseph's objections. Day after day she lay in wait, teasing and tempting him. And still he refused her. Then one day in desperation she cornered Joseph and caught hold of him by the sleeve of his coat. But Joseph was too quick for her, and he made his escape, leaving her with nothing but an empty garment in her hands.

Then Potiphar's wife summoned all the servants. "Look what this Hebrew tried to do!" she said, holding up Joseph's coat. "He forced his way into my bedroom, and when I cried out, he fled, leaving his coat behind." When her husband came home, he was told the same false story. Potiphar, enraged, immediately had Joseph thrown into prison. Fortunately, however, the jailer took a liking to the young man, and put him in charge of all the other prisoners.

It so happened that in the prison with Joseph were Pharaoh's cupbearer and the royal baker. One night each of them had a dream, which in the morning they asked Joseph to explain. "In my dream," said the cupbearer, "I saw a vine with three branches, bearing ripe grapes. I squeezed the juice from these grapes into a cup, which I gave Pharaoh to drink."

"Your dream," said Joseph, "means that in three days Pharaoh will pardon you."

WALL PAINTING
The houses of officials, such as Potiphar, would have been decorated with brightly colored wall paintings like this detail of a hunting scene. Raw materials, such as carbon for black and copper for green, were used as paints.

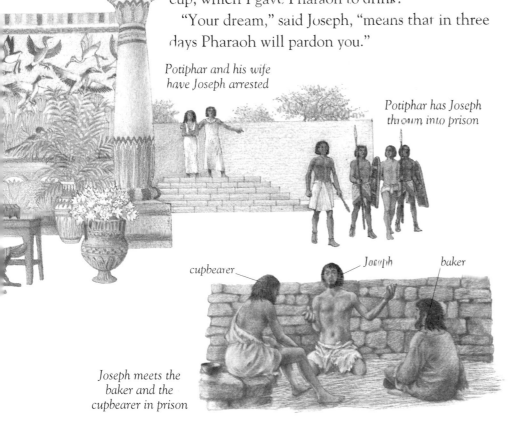

Potiphar and his wife have Joseph arrested

Potiphar has Joseph thrown into prison

cupbearer   Joseph   baker

Joseph meets the baker and the cupbearer in prison

CUPBEARER
This limestone relief shows a cupbearer serving an Egyptian princess. The Pharaoh's cupbearer was a high-ranking official who held an important position of trust. His main duty was to taste food and drink before serving, to check for poison.

"I," said the baker, "dreamed that I had three baskets of bread for Pharaoh stacked on my head, and a flock of birds flew down and ate every crumb."

Joseph looked grave. "I am sorry to say that your dream means that in three days Pharaoh will have you hanged."

And it happened just as Joseph said: within three days the cupbearer was restored to his job, while the baker was hanged.

Pharaoh's Dreams

TWO YEARS HAD PASSED and still Joseph was in jail. Then one night Pharaoh had a strange dream: he was standing by the River Nile and while he watched, seven cows, fat and healthy, came out of the water to feed. A while later seven thin cows came out of the river, so lean and bony they could barely stand. The thin cows ate up the fat cows. Pharaoh woke with a start. Then he fell asleep and dreamed again. This time he saw seven ears of wheat growing plump and golden on a single stalk. Then he saw seven shriveled ears of wheat, which ate up the seven large ears.

In the morning Pharaoh demanded that someone be found to explain his dreams. All the wise men and magicians were brought before Pharaoh, but no one could tell him the meaning of his dreams.

Joseph is brought before Pharaoh and tells him the meaning of his dreams

Pharaoh promotes Joseph to the highest office

Joseph

It was then that the cupbearer remembered Joseph and told Pharaoh how he had correctly interpreted both his and the baker's dreams. Joseph was immediately released from prison and brought before Pharaoh. After thinking for a moment Joseph said, "God has revealed to me what your dreams mean: Egypt is about to enjoy seven years of great plenty, to be followed by seven years of terrible famine. In the time of plenty you must save grain from the harvest and store it, so that there will be enough to eat during the famine."

Pharaoh was so impressed by Joseph that he decided to promote him to the highest office. Pulling the ring from his own finger, he gave it to Joseph, then he hung a heavy gold chain about his neck and dressed him in fine linen robes. He presented him with a magnificent chariot. "You shall be ruler of the whole of Egypt," he declared, "second in power only to myself."

Under Joseph's supervision, grain was gathered and stored during the seven years of good harvest. Then, when the lean years arrived, there was more than enough for all. There was so much that people came from distant lands to buy grain, for the famine was everywhere.

AND JOSEPH GATHERED WHEAT AS THE SAND OF THE SEA, VERY MUCH, UNTIL HE LEFT NUMBERING; FOR IT WAS WITHOUT NUMBER.
GENESIS 41:49

CHARIOT
Egyptian chariots were driven by royalty and high officials, as well as by warriors and hunters. When Pharaoh gave a chariot to Joseph, it was a sign of his new status.

Joseph

Under Joseph's supervision, grain is gathered and stored

Joseph the Governor

Joseph

Simeon is taken prisoner

The brothers kneel down in front of Joseph

FAMINE
This statue of a man with a begging bowl was found in Egypt and dates from the Middle Kingdom around 2000 BCE. It reflects the suffering of ordinary people during times of famine, an ever-present threat in the ancient world. The famine in Egypt would have been caused by a drop in the water level of the River Nile. The river usually provided the Egyptians with plenty of water for their crops.

AND JOSEPH COMMUNED WITH THEM, AND TOOK FROM THEM SIMEON, AND BOUND HIM BEFORE THEIR EYES.
GENESIS 42:24

THE FAMINE HAD SPREAD to Canaan. Joseph's father, Jacob, saw that his people were hungry, so he sent ten of his sons to Egypt to buy wheat. He kept Benjamin, his beloved youngest son, at home with him.

The brothers set off on their long journey from Canaan to Egypt. They found their way to the governor, who was their brother Joseph. Once in his presence they knelt humbly before him, their faces pressed to the ground. Joseph knew at once who they were, but they did not recognize him in his fine clothes.

He spoke accusingly. "You are spies, coming here to spy on Egypt."

"No," they protested. "We are from Canaan, come here to buy grain. We were twelve, but the youngest is at home with our father and one of us is dead."

"Why should I believe you?" Joseph demanded. "You must prove you are not spies. You shall return to Canaan to fetch the youngest. Then I will know if you are telling the truth."

Joseph has his brothers' sacks filled with wheat, and their silver is secretly replaced

On the journey home one of the brothers opens his sack and finds the silver

But first Joseph had the brothers thrown into prison for three days. On the third day they were brought again before him. "Take this wheat back to your land," he said. "But bring your youngest brother here or I shall have you all put to death. And to make sure you obey me, I shall keep one of you here as hostage."

The brothers trembled. They felt guilty and believed that this was a punishment for the way they had treated Joseph.

As they whispered among themselves, Joseph listened, silently weeping at the sight of their frightened faces. He had spoken through an interpreter, and knew they did not realize he could understand everything they said.

Suddenly he gave the order for one of the brothers, Simeon, to be bound in front of them and put in jail. Then he had the sacks of the others filled with wheat, and the silver they had brought to pay for it secretly replaced. Lastly he gave them food before sending them on their way.

Overnight on the journey home one of the brothers opened his sack to get wheat for his donkey, and saw the returned silver. "What does this mean?" they asked each other nervously.

Once back in Canaan they told Jacob everything.

"My children are being taken away from me. First Joseph, then Simeon," said Jacob. "And now you want to take Benjamin. But you shall not take my youngest child from me – if harm came to him I would go to my grave in sorrow."

RECORDING A HARVEST
In Egypt grain was stored in large granaries. Clerks kept a record of stocks, as shown in this Egyptian wall painting. Joseph was a good organizer, and was able to provide his brothers with a supply of wheat from his stores.

PIECES OF SILVER
In the days before coins, silver was often used as money. Joseph's brothers would have paid for their grain with pieces of silver weighed out on scales.

Benjamin and the Silver Cup

WINE FUNNEL
The brothers "drank and were merry" at Joseph's feast. Wine making was commonly practiced in Egypt. Funnels were used to strain the sediment from the wine.

EGYPTIAN FEAST
The Egyptians ate well, and Joseph would have offered his brothers a variety of foods at the feast. This could have included savory dishes of duck, cucumbers, leeks, onions, garlic, and olives, followed by sweet dishes of pomegranates, dates, figs, walnuts, almonds, and wild honey.

Joseph meets his brothers at the feast and weeps at seeing Benjamin

SOON ALL THE GRAIN WAS GONE, and Jacob told his sons that they must go again into Egypt and buy food. "We cannot go without Benjamin," said Judah. Jacob was unhappy, but Judah promised to look after his brother and bring him safely home.

"You must take a present for this all-powerful governor," said Jacob. "Take the best our land has to offer – honey, spices, balm, myrrh – and plenty of silver to pay for the wheat."

Again the brothers went to Joseph, who invited them to eat at his house. There they were welcomed by his steward and joyfully reunited with their brother Simeon. When Joseph entered, they bowed low and laid their presents before him. At the sight of Benjamin, Joseph was so moved that he left the room and wept. On returning, he offered them the best he had in food and wine, and to Benjamin he gave five times more to eat and drink. After dinner Joseph ordered his men to fill the brothers' sacks with grain, and to put back the money they had brought with them. In Benjamin's sack he hid a silver cup of his own.

The brothers left as soon as it was light, but they had not gone far when Joseph's steward caught up with them. He searched their sacks in turn. When the cup was found in Benjamin's sack, the steward had them all arrested and taken back to the city.

SILVER CUPS
These silver cups date from the Middle Kingdom (2133-1786 BCE), the time when the events in the Joseph stories probably took place. The theft of a silver cup was a serious crime because silver was a luxury, which was imported into Egypt from Syria. Also, the cup belonged to Joseph, the governor, second in importance only to the Pharaoh.

steward — | — Benjamin

The silver cup is found in Benjamin's sack

Once more at Joseph's house the brothers threw themselves on the ground, begging for mercy. "You may all go," said Joseph, "except the man in whose sack the goblet was found. He shall stay and be my servant."

"Do not keep Benjamin," Judah implored him. "If he does not return, my father will die of grief, for he loves him dearly, and he has already lost one son. I beg you to keep me instead."

Then Joseph felt his heart would break, and he could bear it no longer. "I am Joseph, your brother, whom you sold as a slave. But now I am Pharaoh's chief adviser and governor of all Egypt. You must come and settle here, for there are five more years of famine to suffer. Bring all you have, your flocks and your herds, and I will look after you. Tell my father what you have seen." And he threw his arms around Benjamin and wept, and then he kissed all his brothers.

The brothers returned to Canaan, and told Jacob that Joseph was alive. Jacob was full of joy at the news. He agreed at once to go with them to Egypt, and there they made their home.

THEY SPEEDILY TOOK DOWN EVERY MAN HIS SACK TO THE GROUND, AND OPENED EVERY MAN HIS SACK. AND HE SEARCHED, AND BEGAN AT THE ELDEST, AND LEFT AT THE YOUNGEST: AND THE CUP WAS FOUND IN BENJAMIN'S SACK.
GENESIS 44:11-12

Life in Egypt

axe   bow   *lyre*   *women in woolen tunics*   *donkey*   *men in woolen kilts*

WHEN JOSEPH'S FAMILY and friends went to live in Egypt, to escape from famine in their own country, they were given land in Goshen, in the north of the country. This area was part of the Nile Delta, where the River Nile breaks up into many smaller rivers before flowing into the Mediterranean Sea. Because there was plenty of water there, the Israelites were able to grow a great many crops.

An Egyptian schoolboy once described in a letter the comfortable way of life:

FROM CANAAN TO EGYPT
The wall paintings above are from an Egyptian tomb at Beni-Hasan. They show a group of people, probably Canaanites, coming into Egypt with their belongings.

"The countryside provides a wealth of good things. Their pools are full of fish, their lagoons are thick with birds, their meadows are covered with green grass. Their storehouses are full of barley and wheat that tower up to the sky. There are onions and chives to season the food, also pomegranates, apples, olives, and figs from the orchards. People are glad to live there."

ON THE NILE
The River Nile (right) was ancient Egypt's greatest asset. Many vegetables and fruits (left) grew in the fertile land of the Nile valley.

Rulers and Slaves

The rulers of Egypt, the pharaohs, were at the center of Egyptian society. They lived in great luxury and built rich palaces, temples, and tombs. They were buried inside huge stone pyramids, with their treasures, often made of gold and silver.

Many Israelites became wealthy and some, like Joseph, who had been sold into slavery, rose to have great influence in Egypt. Then, 300 years after Joseph's time, their fortunes changed. In about 1500 BCE the Egyptian rulers turned against people who had come from other countries: this included the Israelites. They became slaves and had to work for others rather than for themselves.

The Egyptian court was one of the richest of the ancient world.

The Israelites were harshly treated by the Egyptians.

Slaves carried out most of the building work, making bricks from a mixture of mud and straw. Royal buildings were usually made of stone. Israelite slaves may have built the cities of Pithom and Rameses, and the great city of Thebes in the south. The impressive buildings at Thebes and in other parts of Egypt show the skill of builders and craftsmen.

MAP OF THE EXODUS
The route of the Exodus, or exit, from Egypt is not certain. It is likely, however, that the Israelites, led by Moses, avoided the most direct route along the Mediterranean coast so that they did not confront the Philistines in that area.

Moses in Egypt

One of the greatest leaders of the Israelites was Moses, who was found as a baby by the pharaoh's daughter. He grew up in the grand palaces of the Egyptian court and as a boy would have learned to read and write in hieroglyphics and take part in popular sports, such as archery and gymnastics.

Moses left Egypt after he had killed an Egyptian. He never forgot that he was an Israelite, and later he returned to free his people and lead them out of Egypt at God's command.

Moses dies before reaching Canaan

Mt. Nebo

Mediterranean Sea

CANAAN

Rameses

GOSHEN

The ten plagues

Manna from heaven

Water from the rock

Parting of the Red Sea

Ezion-geber

EGYPT

River Nile

Morah

Elim

SINAI

Rephidim

Moses receives God's laws

Red Sea

Moses in the Bulrushes

I N EGYPT A NEW PHARAOH came to the throne. Since Joseph's time, the children of Israel had grown powerful and numerous, and the new king was frightened that they would overrun his country. "We must take precautions against them," he said to his counselors. "If war breaks out, they may side with our enemies and defeat us." First, he gave orders that the Israelites should be treated as slaves, and made to work in gangs, building roads and cities. Then he made a ruling that any male child born to an Israelite woman should immediately be put to death.

Pharaoh rules that any male child born to an Israelite should be put to death

Now there was a young married woman of the tribe of Levi who had recently given birth to a boy. Both parents were delighted, and they made up their minds that their son should escape Pharaoh's cruel command.

For the first three months of the baby's life, his mother managed to hide him in the house. But soon he grew too big to hide, and she knew that she could no longer keep him. With a heavy heart, she made a covered cradle out of dried reeds, which she made watertight by covering it with tar and clay. In this she tenderly placed her baby, and left him hidden among the bulrushes on the banks of the Nile.

All this was watched by the baby's sister, who remained near at hand so that she could see what would happen.

It was not long before Pharaoh's daughter, accompanied by her maids, came down to the river to bathe. Catching sight of the little cradle, she sent one of the girls to bring it to her. As the princess gently removed the cover, the baby began to cry, and her heart was touched. "This must be a Hebrew child," she said.

At that moment, the baby's sister came forward and, curtsying low to the princess, asked if she could be of help. "Shall I find a nurse

GOLDEN FISHES
These lucky charms may have been worn to protect against accidents on the River Nile. Made of gold, children probably wore them in their hair.

BASKET
This Egyptian basket and lid dates from 1400 BCE. Baskets were used as containers for clothes and food in many households. Moses' mother would have found it easy to make one out of papyrus reeds.

from among the Hebrew women to look after the baby?" she said. The princess was delighted with the suggestion, and the girl ran quickly home to fetch her mother.

The princess was happy to employ the woman. "If you will look after the boy," she said, "I will pay you well."

So the baby's real mother was able to bring him up. In time Pharaoh's daughter, who had grown to love the child, adopted him as her son. "I will call him Moses, which means 'to draw out,'" she said, "because I drew him out of the water."

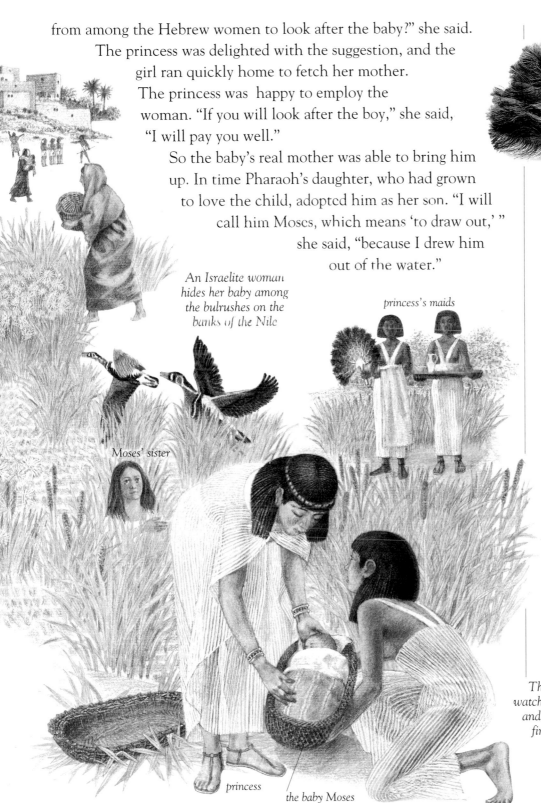

KEEPING COOL
Fans made from ostrich feathers were used by servants, known as fan-bearers, in the Egyptian royal court. This ivory-handled fan dates from the time of Moses (c1300 BCE). Ostriches were a common sight throughout the desert lands of Sinai and Israel in biblical times.

An Israelite woman hides her baby among the bulrushes on the banks of the Nile

princess's maids

Moses' sister

WHEN SHE HAD OPENED IT, SHE SAW THE CHILD: AND, BEHOLD, THE BABE WEPT. AND SHE HAD COMPASSION ON HIM, AND SAID, "THIS IS ONE OF THE HEBREWS' CHILDREN."
EXODUS 2:6

The baby's sister watches as the princess and her servant girl find her brother

princess

the baby Moses

servant girl

Moses Is Called by God

Moses kills an Egyptian for beating an Israelite

MOSES FLED FROM THE FACE OF PHARAOH, AND DWELT IN THE LAND OF MIDIAN: AND HE SAT DOWN BY A WELL.

EXODUS 2:15

MOSES' FLIGHT
Moses fled across the harsh and waterless Sinai Desert before reaching Midian. While tending sheep on Mount Sinai, God appeared to him out of a burning bush. There, Moses was later to receive God's laws.

ALTHOUGH BROUGHT UP AS AN EGYPTIAN, Moses never forgot that he was one of the children of Israel. One day he saw an Egyptian savagely beating an Israelite slave. Looking around to see that no one was watching, he killed the attacker and buried his body in the sand. However, word of what he had done eventually came to Pharaoh's ears, and Moses knew that his life was in danger. He left Egypt and went to the land of Midian.

Presently, he sat down to rest near a well. The seven daughters of Jethro, a priest in Midian, came to the well to draw water. But the local shepherds

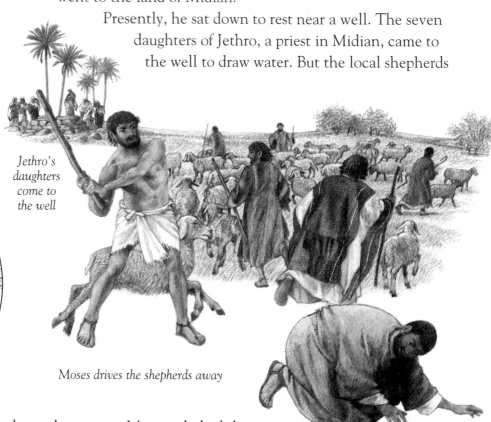

Jethro's daughters come to the well

Moses drives the shepherds away

drove them away. Moses rebuked the men, then helped the young women to fill their jars. When they told their father what had happened, Jethro was so grateful that he gave Moses his daughter Zipporah in marriage.

One day while tending Jethro's sheep, Moses led them far into the desert, to the holy mountain of Sinai. The flock was quietly grazing when suddenly the Lord appeared, from the middle of a bush that had burst into flames. But as Moses looked at the flames licking and crackling among the leaves, he saw that the blazing bush was not being destroyed by the fire.

Then Moses heard the voice of God calling him. "Moses, do not come any nearer, for you are standing on holy ground." At this Moses put his hands over his eyes, for he was afraid to look at God.

"I have seen how my people are suffering in Egypt, where they are treated as slaves," said the Lord. "I will free them from that cruel country and give them a land of their own, a land flowing with milk and honey. You, Moses, must go and bring my people out of Egypt."

"But how am I to do this?" asked Moses.

"I will be with you," said the Lord. "You must tell the Israelites that I am the God of their ancestors, the God of Abraham and Isaac, and they will follow you. Tell them that God, whose name is 'THAT I AM' has sent you.

"You must go to Pharaoh and ask him in my name to release the Israelites. He will be angry and refuse your request. But I will curse Egypt and cause such horrors to fall upon the land that Pharaoh will no longer defy me, and he will let you go."

"But what if they do not believe that I am sent by God?"

"Moses, what are you holding in your hand?"

"A staff," said Moses.

"Throw it to the ground." And Moses threw down his staff, which instantly became a serpent writhing in the dust.

"Now lift it up by the tail."

As Moses picked up the snake, it turned back into a wooden staff.

"Now look at your hand," God commanded him. And Moses saw with horror that his hand was covered with running sores.

"Look again." And Moses looked, and his hand was smooth.

"But Lord, I am slow of speech," said Moses.

"Then your brother Aaron shall speak for you. Now go, do as I have told you, and I will be with you," said God.

A bush bursts into flames in front of Moses and God speaks to him

YAHWEH
The four-letter Hebrew word YHWH was the name which God used to reveal himself to Moses. It is usually written as "Yahweh" and comes from the Hebrew verb "to be." It means "the one who is always there."

Moses Warns the Pharaoh

Pharaoh

Moses

Aaron

Moses and Aaron stand before Pharaoh and ask him to let their people go, but Pharaoh refuses

AFTER GOD HAD SPOKEN TO HIM, Moses returned home. God had told Moses that the men who wanted to kill him were now dead, and it would be safe for him to go back to Egypt. Moses told his father-in-law of his plan, and asked for his blessing. "Go in peace," said Jethro fondly.

So Moses left Midian, taking with him the staff of God. And accompanied by his wife, his sons, and his brother, Aaron, he came once more to Egypt. He and Aaron went at once to see Pharaoh. "I have come at the command of the God of Israel to ask you to let his people go," said Moses.

Pharaoh smiled coldly. "Why do you stir up trouble among my slaves? I will teach you what it means to defy me!" And he gave orders that the Israelites, who had been put to make bricks out of mud and straw, should no longer have straw provided: they must find it for themselves in the fields.

The Israelites, already worked to exhaustion by their masters, were in despair. "How can we make bricks if we must also gather the straw?" they cried. But their cries were ignored, and those who failed to make as many bricks as before were savagely beaten.

"Look at your people, Lord," said Moses. "They are being treated even more harshly, and there is no hope of release."

SLAVERY
The Egyptians generally treated their slaves well, but as the Israelites grew in number the Egyptians felt threatened and dealt with them harshly. They forced them to build their homes and temples and tend their crops and animals in the hot sun. If they did not work long or hard enough, a supervisor punished them.

The Israelites are beaten by their Egyptian masters

Pharaoh

Moses   Aaron

The staffs of Aaron and the royal magicians turn into serpents

PHARAOH

The powerful rulers of Egypt were called pharaohs. This statue is of Rameses II, who ruled Egypt during the 13th century BCE. It is thought that he was the pharaoh to whom Moses spoke. Rameses II was responsible for building more monuments and statues than any other pharaoh. Because of these fine achievements, he is often referred to as Rameses the Great.

"Speak again to Pharaoh," said God. "And demand that he let my people go."

So the brothers stood a second time before Pharaoh and his court, only to receive the same answer. But Moses, remembering what God had told him, signaled to Aaron to throw down the staff. Aaron did so, and as the staff touched the ground it turned into a serpent. At this Pharaoh gave the order to his royal magicians, and they all threw down their staffs, which all turned into serpents. These were swallowed up by Aaron's serpent.

But Pharaoh remained unmoved.

"Go to the banks of the Nile," said the Lord to Moses. "And when Pharaoh comes down to the river, ask him again to let my people go. And if he will not, strike the surface of the water with your staff."

And so Moses and Aaron went down to the river, and waited for Pharaoh to come.

SERPENT

One of the gods worshiped by the Egyptians was the serpent god, Sito, shown above. When Aaron's serpent ate the Egyptian serpents, it showed God's power over the Egyptian gods.

The Plagues of Egypt

ONCE MORE, Moses and Aaron pleaded with Pharaoh to let the people go. When Pharaoh refused to listen, they struck the waters of the River Nile. At once the water turned to blood, and all the fish died, and the dead fish rotted in the sun and stank. For seven days the whole of Egypt ran with blood, and there was no water to drink. But Pharaoh refused to free the Israelites. So Moses and Aaron, following God's

The waters of the Nile turn to blood and all the fish die

command, stretched their sacred staff over the Nile. At once, throughout all Egypt, frogs in their hundreds and thousands came hopping out of rivers, streams, and ponds, hopping into people's houses, into their cupboards and ovens, even into their beds.

Horrified, Pharaoh sent for Moses. "Ask your god to take away this plague," he implored. "And I will let your people go at once!"

Overnight the frogs died. They lay several deep in the villages and fields,

Frogs hop into people's houses

until they were gathered up into evil-smelling heaps.

And when Pharaoh saw that the plague was over, he went back on his word.

Then Aaron struck the sand beneath his feet, and the millions of grains of sand turned into millions of lice that crawled and seethed over every man,

Lice crawl over every man and woman

woman, and beast that lived in the land.

But Pharaoh's heart was like stone.

Next came a cloud of flies: fat, black flies that crawled into people's mouths and under their eyelids.

Again Pharaoh begged Moses, in return for the Israelites' freedom, to rid him of the plague. And when the flies were gone, again he broke his word.

A cloud of flies attacks the people

All the oxen are struck by disease

This time the Lord sent to Egypt disease that killed every horse and camel, all the oxen, the goats, and the sheep, every one.

But still Pharaoh would not let the children of Israel leave.

God said to Moses and Aaron, "Take a handful of ashes

People are covered in boils

from the fire and throw it up into the air." And as they did this, the ashes spread a hideous sickness that broke out in boils, covering the skin of both men and animals.

But Pharaoh was not moved.

Heavy hail flattens whole fields

Then God told Moses to stretch his hand toward the heavens, and instantly there was a crash of thunder, red-hot lightning zigzagged along the ground, and a heavy hail fell from the sky, flattening whole fields and smashing open the trunks of trees.

Pharaoh summoned Moses. "Now I will do as you ask if you will stop the storm." So Moses spoke to the Lord, and the hail and thunder stopped. But the children of Israel were not released.

That same day an east wind began to blow; it blew all day and all night, and with the wind came the locusts. They came in such numbers that the sky was black, and they covered the land so that the land was black, and they ate every remaining blade of grass, every leaf, every fruit left hanging from the tree.

Locusts cover the sky and fields

When Pharaoh repented, God turned the wind, and the locusts were blown into the Red Sea. But God's people were kept captive still.

So God told Moses to stretch out his hand, and darkness fell upon Egypt, and there was no light for three days.

Pharaoh sent for Moses. "Now you may go, you and all your people, but you must leave your flocks behind."

"That I may not do," said Moses.

"Then I shall keep your people as slaves, and I forbid you ever to come into my presence again. If you disobey me in this, you will die."

Darkness falls for three days

The Tenth Plague

*The Israelites daub the doorposts
of their houses with blood*

*In every Egyptian family, the eldest
child draws its last breath and dies*

PASSOVER FEAST
Today, Jewish people
celebrate Passover each
spring. The various foods
symbolize the Exodus:
unleavened bread, a nut
and apple paste called
charoseth, horseradish and
lettuce (the bitter herbs),
a roasted lamb bone,
eggs, and salt water.

THE LORD SPOKE TO MOSES. "I shall bring one last plague to Egypt, a plague so terrible that Pharaoh will have no choice but to let my people go. At midnight tonight every first-born child throughout the country will die. Not one shall escape: all will die, from the firstborn of Pharaoh himself, to the firstborn of the poorest slave, to the firstborn of the cattle in the fields. Only the children of Israel will remain untouched.

"This day shall forever afterward be known as Passover, for tonight I will pass over the whole of Egypt, and my people will be freed. From now on, the day must be kept holy and counted as the first day of the year. Every household must kill a lamb, which shall then be roasted and eaten with bitter herbs and bread that is unleavened. Your doorposts must be daubed with the blood of the slain animal, so that when I pass in the night I shall know to leave untouched the houses marked with blood."

Moses called together all his wise men and counselors and told them what God had said, and how they were to keep this day, the first Passover, holy forever after.

Midnight fell, and suddenly a terrible wailing and screaming was heard, as the Lord passed over the land. Except for the Israelites, not one family was left unharmed. Death was everywhere. Everywhere,

AND PHARAOH CALLED FOR MOSES AND AARON BY NIGHT, AND SAID, "RISE UP AND GET YOU FORTH FROM AMONG MY PEOPLE, BOTH YE AND THE CHILDREN OF ISRAEL; AND GO, SERVE THE LORD, AS YE HAVE SAID."
EXODUS 12:31

Taking all their possessions with them, the Israelites leave Egypt

from Pharaoh's palace to the darkest prison, from the rich merchant's house to the open pasture, the firstborn, both man and beast, drew their last breaths and died.

Pharaoh, rising from his bed in grief, sent for Moses and Aaron. "Take your people and go! Go from my country, and take all your flocks and herds!" By now, the Egyptians were so frightened they begged the Israelites to leave as quickly as possible, and heaped their former slaves with silver, gold, and jewels.

And so it was that after four-hundred-and-thirty years in the land of their captivity, the children of Israel, six-hundred thousand of them, all on foot, men, women, and children, with their flocks and herds and all their possessions, at last left Egypt.

SADDLEBAG
On leaving Egypt, the Israelites may have carried their possessions in saddlebags, similar to this Bedouin one made of goat's hair and wool.

The Crossing of the Red Sea

CROSSING THE SEA
The Hebrew words originally translated as "Red Sea" in fact mean "sea of reeds." It is possible that the Israelites crossed over a marshy swamp to the north of the Red Sea.

THE RED SEA
The Israelites could have camped at a spot like this by the Red Sea. The sea usually looks blue, but when the algae that grow in the water die, the sea becomes a reddish-brown.

GOD LED HIS PEOPLE OUT OF EGYPT and through the wilderness at the edge of the Red Sea. God led them by day as a column of cloud and by night as a column of fire, so they should know which way to go.

But Pharaoh again hardened his heart, angry that he had let his slaves leave. He gave orders to the officers of his army to make ready, and he himself led a force of six hundred chariots, as well as horsemen and foot soldiers, against the Israelites.

The Israelites were camped on the shore when they saw the Egyptian army approaching. They turned in terror to Moses. "Why did you take us from our comfortable captivity only to let us die here in the wilderness?"

"Do not be afraid," Moses reassured them. "The Lord will protect you from harm."

As he spoke, the column of cloud moved over the Egyptians, so that they were in darkness. Then, following the word of the Lord, Moses stretched his hand over the sea. Immediately a strong wind sprang up, and the waters parted, and a passage of dry land appeared along the seabed. Moses led his people along this path, the waters like a high wall on either side of them.

As soon as Pharaoh saw what was happening, he and his army came galloping in pursuit. But as his horsemen and his hundreds of chariots thundered over the dry sand, the Lord commanded Moses again to stretch out his hand. The waters of the Red Sea closed over the Egyptians, and every man was drowned.

But the children of Israel reached the far side of the sea in safety, and when they saw how God had protected them, they gave grateful thanks to God and to the prophet Moses. They sang a song of praise, recalling the happy escape of the children of Israel from their long years of slavery, and their crossing of the Red Sea.

Then Miriam, Aaron's sister, took up her tambourine, and calling the women to follow her, led them in a dance along the water's edge.

THE CROSSING OF THE RED SEA

*The waters of the Red Sea close
over the Egyptians*

*Miriam takes a
tambourine and dances
with the other women*

*Moses and his people cross on dry land and
reach the far side in safety*

God Watches Over the Israelites

Flocks of quails appear in the desert

The Israelites catch the quails and roast them

QUAILS
Migrating quails fly across the Sinai Desert twice a year. Tired from the long flight, they fly low and are easily caught.

MANNA
Some scholars think that the manna may have come from the hammada shrub, above, which grows in southern Sinai. When insects feed on its branches, it produces a sweet, white liquid. Today, Bedouin people use it as a sweetener.

HE ISRAELITES WANDERED in the Sinai Desert for many weeks, hungry and exhausted. They began to whisper against Moses and Aaron. "At least in Egypt we had plenty to eat, but here we may die of starvation."

The Lord heard what they were saying, and told Moses to summon his people. "They shall be well provided with food," God promised.

In the morning the ground is covered with manna from heaven

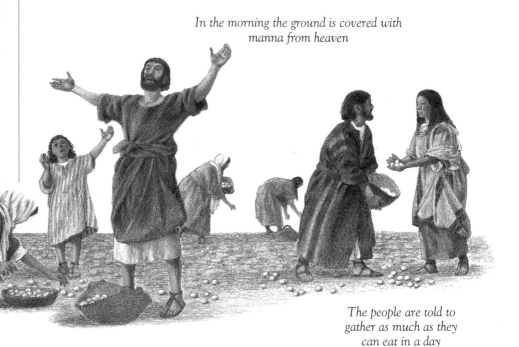

The people are told to gather as much as they can eat in a day

That same evening flocks of quails suddenly appeared, which were caught and roasted.

The next morning the ground was covered with small round shapes, white and tasting of honey. The Israelites were puzzled. "What is this?" they asked each other. "It must be manna, for it falls from Heaven."

"This is bread sent by God," said Moses. "Let the people gather as much as they can eat in a day, and no more." But some were greedy and took more than their share. Secretly they hoarded the manna in their tents, and overnight it turned black, and became full of worms and stank.

On the sixth day, Moses told them they could collect enough food to last for two days. "Tomorrow is a holy day of rest, as decreed by God. Today you must gather up what you need, and eat as much as you want and keep the rest for the Sabbath. It will stay fresh and good overnight, for tomorrow you will find no manna on the ground."

Most people did as Moses said, but a few disobeyed and went out on the Sabbath looking for food.

"When will the people learn to obey my rules?" the Lord asked Moses.

The days passed and the Israelites, as they made their slow way through the burning desert, complained of a lack of water. "Why did you bring us out of Egypt just to die of thirst?" they asked angrily.

But God told Moses to go to a certain rock and strike it with his staff. As he did so, water cold and pure gushed out of the rock, so that all could drink their fill.

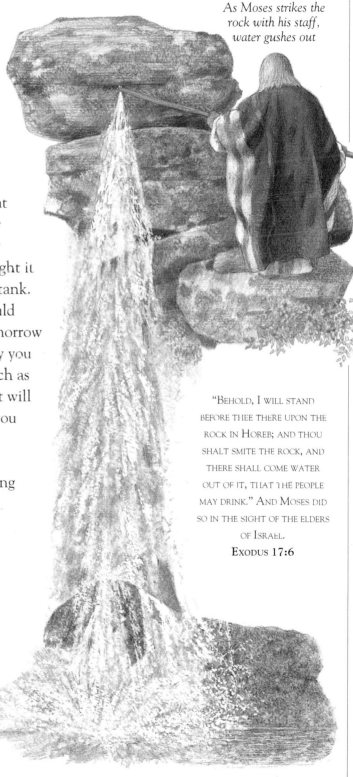

As Moses strikes the rock with his staff, water gushes out

"BEHOLD, I WILL STAND BEFORE THEE THERE UPON THE ROCK IN HOREB; AND THOU SHALT SMITE THE ROCK, AND THERE SHALL COME WATER OUT OF IT, THAT THE PEOPLE MAY DRINK." AND MOSES DID SO IN THE SIGHT OF THE ELDERS OF ISRAEL.
EXODUS 17:6

Moses Receives God's Laws

AND MOSES DREW NEAR
UNTO THE THICK DARKNESS
WHERE GOD WAS.
EXODUS 20:21

AFTER THREE MONTHS the children of Israel arrived at the foot of the holy mountain of Sinai, where they made their camp. Moses went up the mountain to pray to God, who told him that in three days God would speak to the people.

On the morning of the third day the sky turned black, and thunder and lightning crashed and rumbled through the darkness. The mountain itself belched smoke and fire like a great furnace, and the ground shook. Then the voice of God was heard like a mighty trumpet, calling Moses to him.

God calls Moses to him and gives him the ten commandments carved on two stone tablets

"I am the Lord your God, who brought you out of Egypt and these are my commandments, to be obeyed by all my people.

You shall worship no other God but me.

You shall not make any statue or picture to worship.

You shall not speak the name of the Lord except with reverence.

You shall keep the sabbath, the seventh day, as a holy day of rest, for in six days I made the world, but on the seventh day I rested.

You shall show respect to your father and mother.

You shall not commit murder.

You shall not be unfaithful to your husband or wife.

You shall not steal.

You shall not speak falsely against others.

You shall not envy another person's possessions."

When the people heard the thunder and saw the flames and the smoke, they were terrified and would not come near. But Moses reassured them. "Do not be afraid," he said. "God has come to us so that we may learn his commandments and keep ourselves free of sin."

But still the people shrank back, and again Moses went up the mountain alone, to the dark cloud on the summit where God was.

MOUNT SINAI
Moses received God's laws on Mount Sinai, or Mount Horeb, as it is sometimes called in the Bible. Mount Sinai is believed to be the mountain Jebel Musa or "Mountain of Moses," part of a group of peaks in the south of the Sinai Peninsula. It is 7,500 feet (2,300 m) high and is made of red granite.

The Israelites camp at the foot of the holy mountain of Sinai

The Golden Calf

EGYPTIAN BULL GOD
Aaron's golden calf could
have been based on Apis,
an Egyptian bull god
depicted in this painting
from Thebes in Egypt.
Pagan gods were often
represented as bulls in
ancient times. Bulls were
known for their strength
and fearlessness and were
used as symbols of
fertility and power.

AND IT CAME TO PASS, AS
SOON AS HE CAME NIGH UNTO
THE CAMP, THAT HE SAW THE
CALF, AND THE DANCING: AND
MOSES' ANGER WAXED HOT,
AND HE CAST THE TABLES OUT
OF HIS HANDS, AND BRAKE
THEM BENEATH THE MOUNT.
EXODUS 32:19

WHEN THE PEOPLE SAW THAT MOSES had not returned from the mountain, they gathered around Aaron saying, "You must make us a god, for we do not know what has happened to this Moses who brought us out of Egypt."

"Then bring me gold," said Aaron, "and I will give you what you want."

So both men and women brought Aaron their gold jewelry, which he melted down and formed into the shape of a monstrous golden calf. He built an altar to the calf, and the people prayed to it and offered sacrifices, and danced and feasted in front of it.

Looking down from his mountaintop, God said to Moses, "How quickly are my commandments forgotten! Now shall the full force of my anger be felt!"

But Moses begged the Lord to forgive them. "Did you bring them out of Egypt, your chosen people, only to destroy them in your fury?"

Calmed by these words, God sent Moses down the mountain carrying two stone tablets on which were engraved his ten commandments.

As he came near the Israelites' camp, Moses heard loud laughter and music; he saw the statue of the calf, and the smoking sacrificial fires, and drunken figures wildly dancing. Full of anger, he flung the stone tablets to the ground where they broke into pieces. He knocked over the golden idol and threw it on the flames. Then he turned to Aaron. "How could you have let this happen?" he demanded.

Summoning the people together at the entrance of the camp, Moses solemnly addressed them. "Let those who are on the side of the Lord come and stand by me." Only the men of the tribe of Levi went to him, the rest remaining where they were. "Now," he said to the Levites, "go through the camp and with your swords put to death every man you see. For this is the will of God."

Over three thousand men were killed that night, and the next day Moses went again to the Lord to beg forgiveness for his repentant people. "I will send an angel to lead them to the promised land," said God. "But they have made a false idol and must suffer for it."

Aaron builds a
golden calf

The people dance and
feast in front of it

Moses flings the
stone tablets to the
ground in anger

Balaam's Donkey

THE LAND OF MOAB
Balak felt threatened by
the Israelites when they
camped in the plains of
Moab, to the east of the
Dead Sea.

BALAK, KING OF THE MOABITES, looked with fear on the tribes of Israel who were surrounding his land. He sent messengers to the fortune-teller, Balaam, asking him to curse this people so that he might defeat them in battle.

But God had spoken to Balaam. "You must not curse the people of Israel," he said, "for they are my chosen people."

When Balak's messengers arrived, Balaam told them he would not do as they wished.

"If Balak were to give me his own house, every room heaped with gold and silver, still I could not go against the word of God," said Balaam.

But that night God spoke again to Balaam.

"Go with these men, and do just as I tell you."

The next day Balaam saddled his donkey and set

On seeing the angel, Balaam's donkey lies on the ground

Balaam journeys with Balak's messengers to visit Balak in Moab

THE LORD OPENED THE EYES OF
BALAAM, AND HE SAW THE
ANGEL OF THE LORD STANDING
IN THE WAY, AND HIS SWORD
DRAWN IN HIS HAND: AND HE
BOWED DOWN HIS HEAD, AND
FELL FLAT ON HIS FACE.
NUMBERS 22:31

off with Balak's messengers. Suddenly the angel of the Lord appeared, blocking the way, drawn sword in his hand. The donkey saw the angel, and shied away, turning off the road and into a field. But Balaam saw nothing and he beat his mount angrily. Next the angel barred a path that led through a vineyard between high walls. Again the donkey saw him, and squeezed up against the wall, crushing Balaam's foot; and again she was beaten. The angel appeared a third time, standing in the middle of a narrow path where there was no room to turn either to the left or the right. When the donkey saw the angel she lay down on the ground. Balaam was angrier than ever and beat her twice as hard.

Then God gave the animal the power of speech. "Why do you hit me?" she asked. "Because you disobeyed me!" her master furiously replied. "If I had a sword, I would kill you!" Then the Lord opened Balaam's eyes and he saw the angel. Appalled and astonished, he fell flat on his face, begging for forgiveness.

Balak greeted Balaam and took him into the mountains.

BEAST OF BURDEN
The donkey, or ass as it is often called in the Bible, was one of the earliest "beasts of burden." A donkey could carry heavy loads, or burdens, as well as pull the plow.

High on the mountaintop, Balaam blesses the Israelites

Balaam returns to his home in Pethor

Balak is angry with Balaam for disobeying him by not cursing the Israelites

clay bones

model of sheep's liver

TOOLS OF THE TRADE
Balaam was a diviner, or fortune-teller. In ancient times diviners used objects, such as a clay model of a sheep's liver and animal bones, shown above, to make predictions. The bones were thrown down and the pattern they made was studied.

Balaam then went still higher up the mountain where God spoke to him, telling him to bless the Israelites.

Balaam looked down across the wide wilderness and saw the tribes of Israel in their tents and he blessed them. This made Balak very angry. "I called on you to curse my enemies: instead you bless them! I promised you great riches if you would obey me, but now you must go away empty-handed!"

So Balaam returned to his home in Pethor by the River Euphrates.

Life in Canaan

THE BIBLE TELLS US THAT when the Hebrew people escaped from Egypt, they settled in Canaan, the "promised land." Eventually the land they conquered was divided among the 12 tribes, who were the descendants of Jacob, later called Israel. For this reason they were also known as the Israelites. In the valley of the River Jordan, in the east of the country and on the coastal plain in the west, there were many kinds of crops and fruits. Compared to the barren land through which the Israelites had traveled for 40 years, Canaan was a land "flowing with milk and honey."

The Israelites found Canaan a rich and fertile land with many fruits and plentiful crops.

The Israelites were experienced in tending their flocks and living simply off the land, but in Canaan, they found workers skilled in many other crafts and trades. In addition to the farmers, there were stonemasons, potters, builders, metal workers, jewelers, carpenters, and musicians.

The Canaanites were skilled craftsmen.

Canaanite Gods

The Canaanites worshiped many gods and goddesses, including one called Baal. At Ugarit, which is now Ras Sharma in Syria, a statue of Baal was found showing him as a warrior god.

The religion of the Israelites was very different: they worshiped only one God and did not have any statues or carved images. These religious differences led to clashes between the Israelites and the followers of Baal.

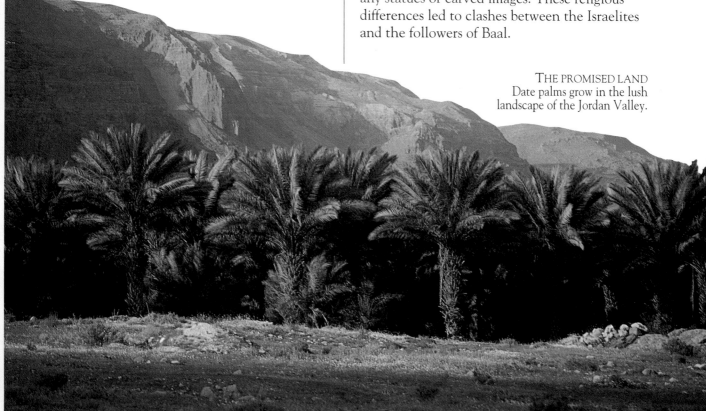

THE PROMISED LAND
Date palms grow in the lush landscape of the Jordan Valley.

The Twelve Tribes of Israel

According to the Bible the 12 tribes of Israel were descended from the 12 sons of Jacob. No tribe was named after Joseph, Jacob's best-known son, but two tribes, Manasseh and Ephraim, took their names from Joseph's sons. Each of the 12 tribes had its own identity and each was given territory when Canaan was conquered. The Levites, who were named after Levi, had no territory, because they were responsible for organizing and carrying out the worship of God in the tabernacle, the sacred meeting tent.

Judges and Kings

To begin with, the Israelites did not have a king. They were linked by the law of God given to them by Moses and by their understanding and worship of God. Moses appointed judges to make sure that the people lived according to God's laws. Later these judges became leaders of the people.

The Bible tells us that when they were being attacked by their chief enemy, the Philistines, the Israelites decided that they wanted a central government, to be ruled by a king. As a result, Saul became the first king of Israel. He was succeeded by his son-in-law David and David's son Solomon.

Saul

The map above shows the kingdoms of the 12 tribes of Israel, each with its own emblem, or symbol.

Later the kingdom was divided into two: Israel, in the north, ruled by a series of kings beginning with Jeroboam, and Judah in the south, ruled by Solomon's descendants, beginning with his son Rehoboam. Israel was destroyed by the Assyrians after 200 years, but Judah (from which the word Jew comes) lasted for another 135 years before Jerusalem was destroyed by the Babylonians and the people taken to live in exile in Babylon.

THE KINGS OF ISRAEL AND JUDAH

Saul   David   Solomon

Rehoboam

Jeroboam

King Saul was succeeded by David and then Solomon. On Solomon's death the kingdom was split between Rehoboam and Jeroboam.

The Promised Land

ROM HIS CAMP IN THE PARAN DESERT, Moses sent twelve men to spy out Canaan, the land which God had promised to the people of Israel. The men carefully explored the country, and after forty days returned, bringing with them handfuls of grapes, figs, and pomegranates.

"It is a rich country flowing with milk and honey," they told Moses and Aaron. "But the people are strong and they live in great walled cities. We would never be able to overcome them."

In spite of this report, Caleb, from the tribe of Judah, was eager to invade at once and take possession of the country. But the others,

CLUSTER OF GRAPES
The large, juicy grapes brought back from Canaan were important to the Israelites. Grapes could be eaten fresh, dried as raisins, boiled to make grape syrup, or pressed to make wine.

AND THEY TOLD HIM, "WE CAME UNTO THE LAND WHITHER THOU SENTEST US, AND SURELY IT FLOWETH WITH MILK AND HONEY."
NUMBERS 13:27

The men return from Canaan, bringing with them grapes, figs, and pomegranates

Moses *Joshua*

*Moses calls Joshua and says that he must
lead the people into Canaan*

AND MOSES CALLED UNTO
JOSHUA AND SAID UNTO HIM
IN THE SIGHT OF ALL ISRAEL,
"BE STRONG AND OF A GOOD
COURAGE: FOR THOU MUST GO
WITH THIS PEOPLE UNTO THE
LAND WHICH THE LORD HATH
SWORN UNTO THEIR FATHERS
TO GIVE THEM."
DEUTERONOMY 31:7

who had been with him on the expedition, were afraid. "We would be defeated," they said. And to make their argument convincing, they pretended they had seen a race of giants in Canaan, beside whom the Israelites would look like grasshoppers.

For forty years the children of Israel continued to wander in the wilderness. In time Aaron died, and Moses knew that he, too, would soon die. He called Joshua, son of Nun, and said, "I am old and will never reach Canaan. You must lead our people there. Be strong and of good heart. Do not be afraid, for God will be with you."

Then Moses inscribed the law of God on two tablets of stone, for he knew that without his guidance the Israelites would soon take to evil ways. The priests kept the tablets in a golden chest called the Ark of the Covenant, which had been made as a holy resting place for the ten commandments.

Having blessed his people, Moses went to the summit of Mount Pisgah where God showed him the whole of the promised land, stretching from Gilead, Dan, Judah, and the distant sea in the west to the southern valley of Jericho, city of palm trees.

There Moses died and was buried, and the people wept for thirty days. Since his death there has never been a prophet like him in Israel. He was a man who had the courage to defy Pharaoh and lead his people out of Egypt; a man who stood face to face with God.

CANAAN
In the northern part of Canaan is the valley of Jezreel (pictured here). Although known as a land "flowing with milk and honey", Canaan is a land of variety. The area descends from fertile hills and fields to a barren desert watered by springs.

Moses is shown the promised land before he dies

Rahab and the Spies

JOSHUA LED HIS PEOPLE to the River Jordan, which was all that divided them from the promised land. He sent two men as spies across the river and into the city of Jericho. There, they were hidden in the house of a woman called Rahab.

The king of Jericho had heard reports that spies were in the city, and he gave orders for every street and every house to be searched. When his officers came to Rahab's door, she, having hidden the two Israelites under some flax on her roof, swore that there was no one inside. The danger over, she said to the men, "Because I have saved your lives, you must swear by the Lord that no harm will come to any member of my family."

"We swear," they said. And it was agreed that Rahab should tie a scarlet thread to her window so that the invaders would know not to attack her house. Then, Rahab let the spies down by a rope, and they escaped into the night.

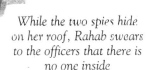

While the two spies hide on her roof, Rahab swears to the officers that there is no one inside

FLAX
Flax plants were grown for making linen. The plants were picked and the stems placed in water to separate the fibers. They were left to dry on flat roofs, like Rahab's. A comb was used to separate the threads. These were then woven together to make linen.

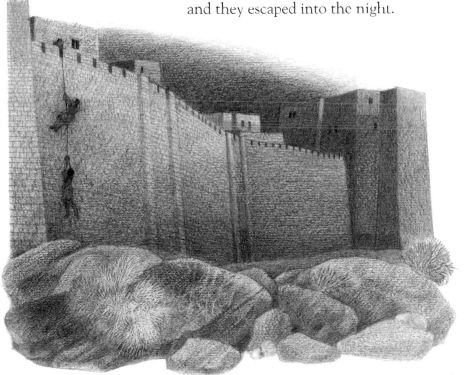

Rahab lets the spies down by a rope

The Battle of Jericho

The priests carry the Ark of the Covenant across the River Jordan, which had stopped flowing

FTER THE TWO MESSENGERS had returned from Jericho, they reported to Joshua, and he assembled all his people on the banks of the Jordan. "Listen carefully to what I have to say. As soon as the priests carrying the Ark of the Covenant put their feet in the water, the river will stop flowing. The waters coming from the source will cease, and a path of dry land will appear. On this you will all be able to cross safely to the other side." And it happened exactly as Joshua had described. The people left their tents and came down to the riverbank; the priests lifted up the Ark and approached the water. At once the waters stopped and divided, and the priests walked to the middle of the riverbed. There they stood, holding the Ark up high, while all of Joshua's people passed safely to the far side. The priests

The Israelite army circles the city

The seven priests blow their trumpets made from rams' horns

"WHEN THEY MAKE A LONG BLAST WITH THE RAM'S HORN, AND WHEN YE HEAR THE SOUND OF THE TRUMPET, ALL THE PEOPLE SHALL SHOUT WITH A GREAT SHOUT; AND THE WALL OF THE CITY SHALL FALL DOWN FLAT."
JOSHUA 6:5

then followed, and no sooner had they stepped onto dry land, than the waters closed over behind them.

Joshua then gathered his army together. Over forty-thousand men stood ready to fight on the plains of Jericho. All of them were willing to die for Joshua, for he was as inspiring a leader as Moses: his people both trusted him and feared his anger, for they knew that, like Moses, he was loved by God.

Jericho was in a state of siege, the gates bolted shut against the Israelite army. The Lord said to Joshua, "Each day for six days you and all your men shall walk once around the city walls. The Ark shall be carried behind you, led by seven priests holding trumpets made out of rams' horns. On the seventh day, you shall circle the city seven times, the priests shall blow their trumpets, and the people shout to the skies. Then will the walls of Jericho fall to the ground. All who live in the city will be killed except for Rahab and her family and household. They shall be spared, because it was she who hid our messengers."

And so it happened. Joshua warned his men not to make a sound for six days; but on the seventh day, as they walked for the seventh time around the city, Joshua said to his people, "Shout! For the Lord has given this city to you."

And so the Israelites raised a great shout, the priests blew their trumpets, and the walls of Jericho fell to the ground. Every man, woman, and child in the city was killed: only Rahab and those living in her house survived.

SHOFAR
Joshua's men would have steamed a ram's horn to make it soft, and then bent the wide end to form a trumpet, or *shofar*. The deep, mournful sounds of this horn are still heard in Jewish synagogues on certain holy days, such as the Day of Atonement, when the people think about the wrongs they have done.

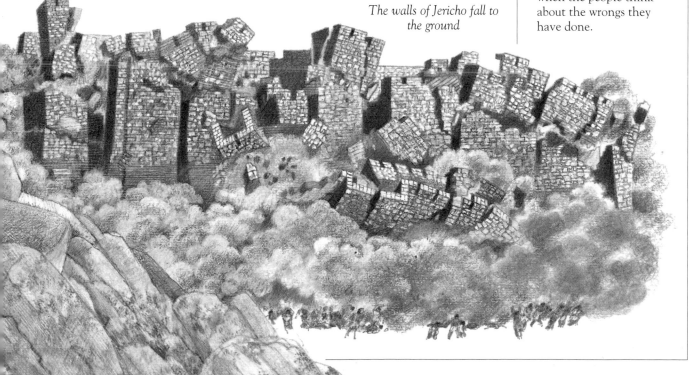

The walls of Jericho fall to the ground

The Call of Gideon

THE ISRAELITES HAD A NEW AND POWERFUL ENEMY, the people of Midian. As soon as the grain was ready for harvest, the Midianites would attack, burning the wheat and slaughtering the animals. The Israelites had begun to worship other gods, but in their despair they appealed to God for help.

The Lord sent an angel to Gideon. "It is you who must save your people from this scourge," said the angel. Gideon, hot and tired from threshing the small amount of wheat he had managed to hide, looked at the angel in astonishment. "But I am only a poor farmer," he said.

"The Lord will be with you," the angel assured him.

That night, in obedience to God's word, Gideon smashed the altar that had been built to the god Baal. In its place he put up an altar to the Lord. The next morning the Israelites gathered around the fallen altar. "Who has done this terrible thing?" they demanded.

Soon it became known that Gideon was the man. "He must die!" shouted the crowd. But Gideon's father said, "If Baal is a god, then let

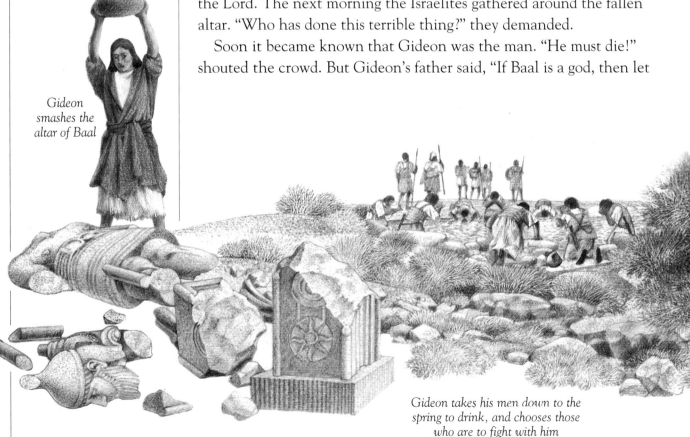

Gideon smashes the altar of Baal

Gideon takes his men down to the spring to drink, and chooses those who are to fight with him

96

him take his own revenge!" And to this the people agreed.

Gideon then gathered his forces and pitched camp by the spring of Harod. "If there are any among you who are afraid, let them go now," he commanded. At these words, over half his army of twenty-two thousand men turned for home. Then God told him to take the remaining ten thousand men down to the spring, and watch how they drank. God said to Gideon: "Those who cup the water in their hands, keep with you; but those who put their faces into the water, send away."

At last, with a company of only three hundred, Gideon looked down on the Midianite army camped in the valley below. When darkness fell, he gave each of his men a trumpet made of ram's horn and a flaming torch covered by an earthenware jar. Silently the army of Israelites surrounded the enemy camp, and at a signal from Gideon, blew their trumpets, smashed the jars to reveal the light from the torches, and shouted as loud as they could. Confused and terrified, the Midianites began fighting each other as they fled into the night.

So Gideon won his victory without striking a single blow.

SPRING OF HAROD
At God's command, Gideon watched to see how his soldiers drank from the waters of this spring. Those who cupped the water in their hands, rather than put their faces in the water, were chosen to fight. One interpretation is that God chose those who were the most alert and ready for battle.

Gideon's army
attacks the
Midianites at night

Jephthah's Daughter

EPHTHAH WAS THE SON OF GILEAD, but as he did not share the same mother as his brothers, they resented him and eventually turned him out of the house, telling him he was not a worthy member of the family. Knowing he would not be allowed to stay near them, Jephthah went to live in the land of Tob.

Time passed, and the Ammonites declared war on the children of Israel. Having heard of his courage and skill as a soldier, the Israelites went to Jephthah and asked him to return; they begged him to be their general and lead them in battle against the enemy.

"But I was turned away from my home," said Jephthah. "Why do you

AMMONITE HEAD
This limestone statue shows the head of an Ammonite king. The Ammonites lived in eastern Canaan from about 1200 BCE to 600 BCE. Because they were descended from Lot, the Israelites left them in peace at first, but the Ammonites later became their sworn enemies.

Jephthah promises God he will sacrifice whatever he sees first if he is given victory over the Ammonites

TIMBREL
A timbrel is a kind of tambourine made from skins stretched over a wooden hoop. Israelite women played timbrels in feasts and processions while chanting God's praises, or to celebrate the return of war heroes.

come to me? I am no longer one of you."

Eventually, however, they persuaded him and he agreed to go back as commander of the army.

First, he sent a messenger to the Ammonite king demanding that he withdraw his troops from Canaan. But the king refused. So then Jephthah prayed to the Lord. "O God, if you will give me victory over the Ammonites, I will sacrifice to you whatever I first see on reaching home."

With Jephthah as their leader, the Israelites easily defeated the enemy. Many Ammonites were killed, and the rest ran for their lives.

Jephthah arrived home, where his only child, his daughter, came running out of the house to greet him. She was brightly dressed, and

Jephthah's daughter weeps with her friends for the life she is about to leave

Jephthah tears his clothes in grief when his daughter runs out to meet him

danced around him, laughing and shaking her timbrel. But her father tore his clothes in grief and covered his face in his hands and sobbed. "I have made a promise to God. I cannot go back on my word, but if I keep it, you, my daughter, will die!"

"You must keep your promise," she said. "The Lord has given you victory over the enemy, and it is right that you fulfill your side of the bargain. But let me have a few weeks to prepare for what is to come." So for two months she wandered the mountains with her friends, and wept for the life that she was about to leave. Then she returned to her father, and he sacrificed her, according to the vow he had made.

AND JEPHTHAH CAME TO MIZPEH UNTO HIS HOUSE, AND, BEHOLD, HIS DAUGHTER CAME OUT TO MEET HIM WITH TIMBRELS AND WITH DANCES: AND SHE WAS HIS ONLY CHILD.
JUDGES 11:34

Samson and the Lion

FOR FORTY YEARS the children of Israel had suffered at the hands of the Philistines, a fierce enemy from the lands near the sea. Then an angel appeared to an Israelite couple who had long been childless. "You will have a son who will win a great victory over the Philistines," the angel told them. "But you must be careful never to cut his hair." The angel then warned the woman. "While you are carrying the child, you must not touch wine or any strong drink, for your son will be a Nazirite, and his life will be dedicated to God."

LION
Lions were the most dangerous animals living in Canaan. They roamed wild in forests and thickets, and were a threat to other animals and people. Samson was so strong, he killed a lion with his bare hands.

Samson kills a lion, tearing it apart with his hands

The child was called Samson, and he grew tall and strong. One day Samson said to his father, "Father, I have seen a beautiful Philistine woman at Timnah, and I want her for my wife." His parents were unhappy that he had chosen a Philistine. "There are many Hebrew women who would make you a good wife: will you not look among them first?" But when they saw that Samson was determined, they did not stand in his way.

Samson and his parents went to Timnah, and as they walked through the vineyards a young lion leapt out at them. As easily as if he were swatting a fly, Samson killed it, tearing it apart with his hands. Then he went to the woman's house and they talked together, and she delighted Samson. It was not long before he asked her to marry him. A little later, he saw in the lion's carcass a honeycomb covered in bees; this he scooped out and ate as he walked, with no thought of being stung. He gave some to his parents, but did not say how he had come by it.

Samson eats honey, found in the lion's carcass

To celebrate his wedding he invited thirty of his wife's friends to a feast, which was to last seven days, for this was the custom of the country. On the first day, he put a riddle to his guests, promising rich rewards to anyone who could answer it. "Out of the eater comes meat; out of the strong comes sweet: what does this mean?" No one could guess. For three days they puzzled over it until finally one of the Philistines went to Samson's wife. "You must make your husband tell you the answer, or we will burn your house to the ground!"

Very frightened, Samson's wife went to him weeping. "How can you say you love me if you will not tell me the solution to your riddle? It is not much to ask!"

"I shall tell nobody," said Samson. "Not even you." But his wife coaxed and cried, until on the seventh day he told her. At once she ran to her friends with the news. And when that evening Samson again put the riddle, one of them stood up. "I can answer that!" he shouted. "There is nothing sweeter than honey. There is nothing stronger than a lion." Samson, realizing he had been tricked, was very angry. In his rage he killed thirty Philistines. Then he returned to his father's house and never saw his wife again.

BRAIDED HAIR
Samson was a Nazirite, a person dedicated to God. Nazirites had to promise never to cut their hair. Samson wore his uncut hair braided, like the prince in the stone sculpture above.

Samson and Delilah

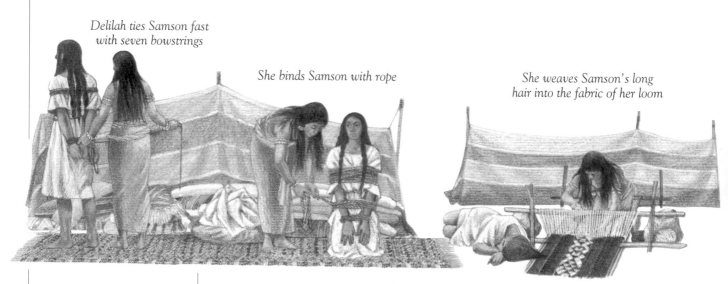

Delilah ties Samson fast with seven bowstrings

She binds Samson with rope

She weaves Samson's long hair into the fabric of her loom

DELILAH SAID TO SAMSON, "TELL ME, I PRAY THEE, WHEREIN THY GREAT STRENGTH LIETH."
JUDGES 16:6

WEAVING
In weaving, threads are intertwined to make cloth. This nomadic woman is weaving on a horizontal loom, similar to the one Delilah would have used.

TIME PASSED, AND SAMSON fell in love with a woman called Delilah. The Philistine lords went to Delilah and told her she must uncover the secret of Samson's great strength. "Find out how we may take him prisoner, and each one of us will give you eleven-hundred pieces of silver."

When Delilah was alone with Samson, she questioned him prettily.

"Tell me, what is the secret of your strength? And how could you be made captive?"

"If I were bound with seven new bowstrings, then I should be helpless as a child," Samson replied.

As if in play, Delilah then tied him fast with seven bowstrings given her by the Philistines, who were lying in wait in the next room. "The Philistines are upon us!" she cried. But Samson snapped the strings as easily as if they had been frail threads.

"Why did you not tell me the truth?" Delilah asked crossly.

"The truth?" said Samson. "The truth is that I can be held only by ropes that have never been used."

As before, Delilah bound him fast, and as before the Philistines burst in upon them, only to see Samson break the ropes as easily as if they had been spun of spider webs.

The third time Delilah put her question, Samson told her that if she wove his long hair into the fabric on her loom, then he would be weak. But again, when the Philistines tried to lay hands on him, he broke away effortlessly.

"How can you say you love me," sobbed Delilah, "when you tell me nothing but lies!" And she needled and nagged him until at last Samson, sick to death of her pestering, told his secret. "If my hair is cut, then my strength is gone."

Delilah watches as the Philistines arrest Samson

Samson is led away in shackles

PHILISTINE HEADDRESS
The Philistines lived along the Mediterranean coast in southwest Canaan from 1200 BCE to 600 BCE. They had a well-organized army. The soldiers wore distinctive feathered headdresses, as shown in the stone carving above, which made them appear very tall. They fought with iron swords and spears.

He fell asleep, exhausted, on her lap; and while he slept Delilah signaled to one of the Philistines, who crept in and cut off the strong man's hair. "Samson, the Philistines are upon us!" she cried. And Samson, not knowing that his strength had left him, jumped to his feet; but at once was overpowered.

His captors blinded him, and took him to Gaza where he was thrown into prison. There brass shackles were locked around his ankles, and he was put to work grinding wheat. But slowly his hair began to grow.

SAMSON TOLD DELILAH ALL HIS HEART, AND SAID UNTO HER, "THERE HATH NOT COME A RAZOR UPON MINE HEAD; FOR I HAVE BEEN A NAZIRITE UNTO GOD FROM MY MOTHER'S WOMB: IF I BE SHAVEN, THEN MY STRENGTH WILL GO FROM ME, AND I SHALL BECOME WEAK, AND BE LIKE ANY OTHER MAN."
JUDGES 16:17

Samson in the Temple

Samson pushes against the pillars of the temple

THE PHILISTINES WERE IN THE TEMPLE celebrating and offering sacrifices to their god, Dagon. "Thanks be to Dagon, for he has delivered the enemy into our hands!" they chanted. As the singing and dancing became louder and wilder, there were shouts for Samson.

"Bring him out! Let us see the Israelite champion! Where is his strength now!"

The blind prisoner was led into the temple and put to stand between the pillars of the doorway, so that everyone could see him. The crowd grew from hundreds to thousands, all of them laughing and jeering at Samson's helplessness.

"O Lord God, give me my strength once more!" Samson silently entreated.

Bracing his hands against the pillar on either side of him, Samson pushed with all his might. There was a noise as though the earth were cracking open, and suddenly the temple, roof and walls, crashed to the ground, killing everyone inside it, including Samson.

So, in dying, Samson won a final victory over the Philistines.

AND SAMSON CALLED UNTO THE LORD, AND SAID, "O LORD GOD, REMEMBER ME, I PRAY THEE, AND STRENGTHEN ME, I PRAY THEE, ONLY THIS ONCE, O GOD, THAT I MAY BE AT ONCE AVENGED OF THE PHILISTINES FOR MY TWO EYES."
JUDGES 16:28

The temple comes crashing down on the Philistines

Ruth and Naomi

Orpah returns to Moab, while Ruth
and Naomi journey together to
Bethlehem

Boaz watches Ruth working in his field

Orpah   Ruth   Naomi

BETHLEHEM
Ruth and Naomi would
have traveled from Moab
for about 50 miles
(80 km) before reaching
Bethlehem. The town is
set high up on a hill and
is surrounded by fertile
fields. Bethlehem is the
birthplace of David.

FOR MANY YEARS the widow Naomi had made her home
in Moab. Her husband had died there, and so had her
two sons. Their wives, Orpah and Ruth, lived with
her. During a time of famine, Naomi decided to return to her
own country, to Bethlehem. "We will come with you," said
her daughters-in-law.

"No," said Naomi. "Your place is not with me, an old woman. You
must stay in Moab where you belong."

Orpah was content with this, but Ruth loved Naomi and would not
be parted from her. "Where you go, there shall I follow," she said.
"Your home shall be mine; your people, my people; your God, my
God." And so Ruth and Naomi journeyed together to Bethlehem.

They arrived at harvest time, and Ruth went into the fields to
gather the leftover barley. Boaz, a cousin of Naomi's, who owned the
fields, noticed the young woman and asked who she was. He was

Ruth gathers the barley that is left over

HARVESTING
The picture above shows women cutting and gathering grain during harvest time. Poor people, like Ruth, would come later to collect any leftover grain. This is known as gleaning.

While Boaz sleeps, Ruth lies down at his feet

touched to hear about her kindness to Naomi, and went over to her. "Come and eat with us. You are safe here with my people."

That evening Naomi told Ruth to return to Boaz. "Wait until he has fallen asleep, then go quietly and lie down beside him."

As soon as she saw that Boaz slept, Ruth lay down at his feet. In the middle of the night, he woke with a start and saw the form of a woman in the darkness. "Who are you?"

"I am Ruth, and I have come to ask for your protection."

"There is someone closer to you in the family than I: but if he does not wish to look after you and Naomi, then I shall take care of you."

And so it turned out. Ruth and Boaz were married, and Ruth gave birth to a son, who brought great happiness to Naomi in her old age.

WHEN BOAZ HAD EATEN AND DRUNK, AND HIS HEART WAS MERRY, HE WENT TO LIE DOWN AT THE END OF THE HEAP OF WHEAT: AND SHE CAME SOFTLY, AND UNCOVERED HIS FEET, AND LAID HER DOWN.
RUTH 3:7

Samuel Is Called to Serve God

H ANNAH WAS ONE of the two wives of Elkanah. Penninah had children, but even though Elkanah loved her, Hannah had none. Every year they went to pray at Shiloh, where the Ark of the Covenant was kept, and every year Penninah would mock Hannah because she had no children. One night Hannah went to the temple and prayed to God. "Lord, please send me a son, and I promise to devote his life to your service."

Eli, the high priest, watched her praying, then he blessed her as she left. "May God grant your wish," he said.

In due course Hannah gave birth to a son, whom she called Samuel.

Eli watches as Hannah prays to God for a son

Hannah gives her son, Samuel, to Eli to look after

BREASTPIECE
Eli was a high priest and would have worn a linen breastpiece like the one above. It is inset with 12 gemstones, representing the 12 tribes of Israel. The breastpiece was tied to an *ephod*, a two-piece apron, which the high priest wore over his blue robe.

TEACHING THE LAW
As a high priest, Eli would have taught Samuel to obey God's laws. In the same way, a rabbi – a teacher of Jewish laws – instructs the young today.

Hannah nursed the child, then, not forgetting her promise to God, she took Samuel to the temple and gave him to Eli to look after. Every year, when she came with her husband to pray at Shiloh, Hannah brought with her a little coat for Samuel. Eli cared for him lovingly and brought him up to obey God's word. The child grew as straight and true as Eli's own two sons were dishonest and sly.

One night Samuel was awakened by a voice calling his name. "Here I am," he said, and jumping from his bed ran to see what Eli wanted.

"I did not call you," said the old man. "Go back to bed."

But in a short while the boy heard the voice again – "Samuel, Samuel!" – and again he went in to Eli, but the priest assured him that he had not spoken. The third time Samuel heard the voice, Eli told him that it must be the voice of God.

So Samuel lay down in the dark and waited. "Samuel, Samuel."

"Lord," the child replied. "I am your servant, and ready to listen."

"The sons of Eli are evil men. You must tell their father that they cannot serve as priests or be pardoned for their wickedness."

The next morning Samuel told Eli what God had said. "So be it," said Eli. "It is the word of the Lord."

The Lord came, and stood, and called as at other times, "Samuel, Samuel." Then Samuel answered, "Speak; for thy servant heareth."

I Samuel 3:10

While Eli sleeps, Samuel is awakened by a voice calling him

The Ark Is Captured

THE ISRAELITES, badly defeated in battle by the Philistines, decided to fetch the Ark of the Covenant from Shiloh. When the Ark was near they believed that God was with them, and would save them from their enemies. The Ark was carried into the camp and a great shout went up, a shout that struck fear into the hearts of the Philistines.

"The Israelite God is a terrible god," they said to one another.

*The Philistines find the statue of Dagon
lying broken next to the Ark*

"We must fight with all our strength not to be overcome." And again the Philistines fought and defeated the people of Israel, and then they seized the Ark.

A man from the tribe of Benjamin fled from the battle and went to Shiloh where he found Eli, the old priest.

"What has happened, my son?" asked Eli.

"The Philistines have defeated us, we have suffered heavy losses, and the Philistines have taken the Ark."

When Eli heard that the Ark of the Covenant – which he had watched over for so many years – had been captured, his heart stopped and he fell to the ground dead.

The Philistines took the Ark to Ashdod, and put it in the temple of Dagon beside a statue of their god. The next morning, the statue of

DAGON
The chief god of the
Philistines was Dagon,
god of grain and fertility.
He is sometimes
represented as part fish,
part man, as shown here.

Dagon was found lying on the ground in front of the Ark. Puzzled, the priests set the golden image upright, but the following day Dagon was found again on the ground, with his head and both hands broken off. Soon afterward the Philistines were struck by a plague of boils, and their land was overrun with rats.

"We must send the Ark back with a peace offering," they decided. They laid the Ark on a cart, and beside it they placed a casket of gold. They wanted to see how powerful the God of the Israelites was, so they put untrained cows between the shafts and, without a driver, the cows pulled the cart straight down the road. Some Israelites were harvesting wheat in the fields when they looked up and saw the cart approaching. Overjoyed, they ran to it and gently lifted the sacred chest to the ground. A burnt sacrifice was made, and they thanked God that the Ark was safely in their hands once more.

OX AND CART
The Israelites used trained oxen to pull simple wooden carts, like the one in the picture above. Valued for their strength, oxen were also used for plowing and threshing

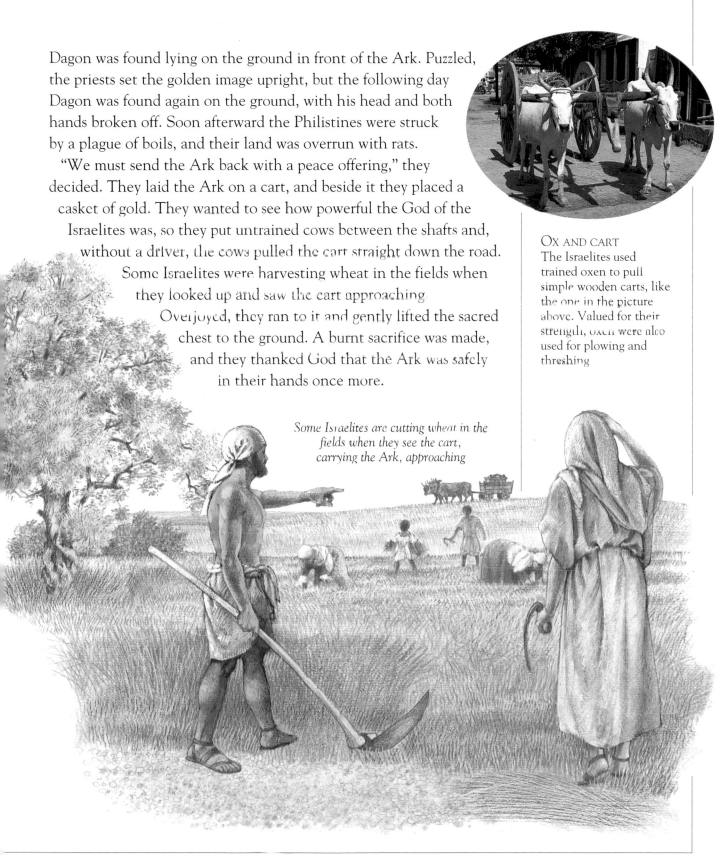

Some Israelites are cutting wheat in the fields when they see the cart, carrying the Ark, approaching

Saul, the First King of the Israelites

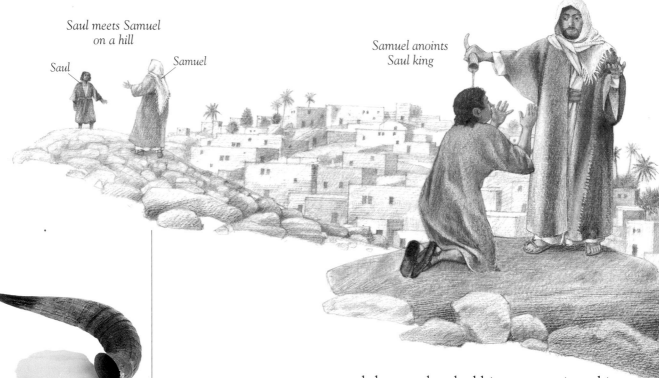

*Saul meets Samuel
on a hill*

Saul

Samuel

*Samuel anoints
Saul king*

HORN AND OIL
Samuel anointed Saul
king with oil contained
in an animal's horn. It
was a sign that Saul was
chosen by God and
belonged to the Lord in a
special way. Samuel
would have used olive
oil, perfumed with spices
and myrrh. The Israelites
had many other uses for
oil. They used it in
cooking, to soothe cuts
and bruises, for preparing
a body for burial, and as
fuel for lamps.

SAMUEL GREW OLD, and the people asked him to appoint a king
to rule over them. Samuel asked God what he should do.

"There is a man called Saul, of the tribe of Benjamin, and
he is the one you must choose. He will make himself known to you."

Shortly afterward, a tall young man came up to Samuel on a hill
outside the city. "I have lost three of my donkeys," he said. "I know
you are a prophet: can you tell me where they are?"

"Your donkeys are safe," Samuel replied. "Now come with me, for
you are to be the first king of Israel." Saul was astonished. "But I am
unimportant!" he exclaimed. "I am of the tribe of Benjamin, the
smallest of all the tribes of Israel, and my family is the least important
family in the tribe." Samuel reassured him, and led the astonished
Saul back to his house, where he gave him food and then anointed
him with oil, pouring it over his head.

"With this oil," he said, "I declare you king. Now you must return
home. On your way you will see two men who will tell you your
donkeys are found. Next you will meet three men, the first leading

three young goats, the second carrying three loaves of bread, the third a bottle of wine; they will give you two of their loaves. Lastly, you will come across a group of prophets making music and singing praises to God, and you will join with them."

Everything happened exactly as predicted, after which Samuel called the children of Israel together. "I am here to show you your king," he told them. "Where is Saul, of the tribe of Benjamin?" But Saul, overwhelmed, was hiding among some baggage. He was soon found, however, and brought before Samuel, where he stood head and

SAMUEL SAID TO ALL THE PEOPLE, "SEE YE SAUL WHOM THE LORD HATH CHOSEN, THAT THERE IS NONE LIKE HIM AMONG ALL THE PEOPLE?" AND ALL THE PEOPLE SHOUTED, AND SAID, "LONG LIVE THE KING!"
1 SAMUEL 10:24

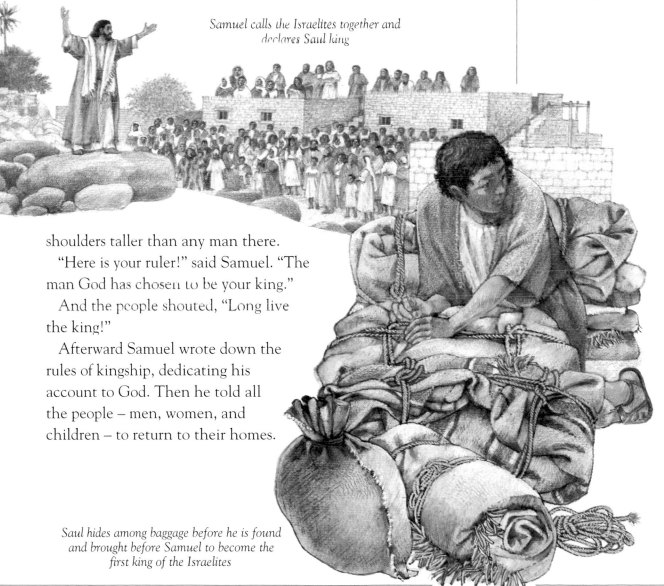

Samuel calls the Israelites together and declares Saul king

shoulders taller than any man there.

"Here is your ruler!" said Samuel. "The man God has chosen to be your king."

And the people shouted, "Long live the king!"

Afterward Samuel wrote down the rules of kingship, dedicating his account to God. Then he told all the people – men, women, and children – to return to their homes.

Saul hides among baggage before he is found and brought before Samuel to become the first king of the Israelites

Saul's Downfall

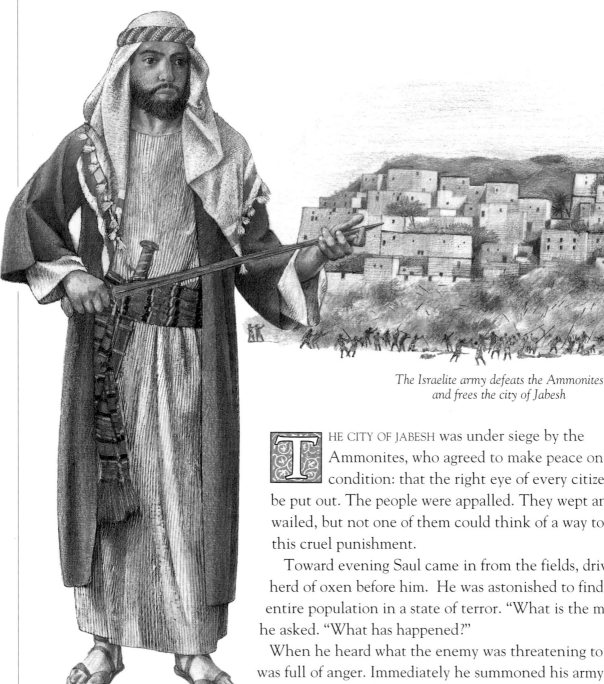

The Israelite army defeats the Ammonites and frees the city of Jabesh

Saul summons his entire army to attack the Ammonites

THE CITY OF JABESH was under siege by the Ammonites, who agreed to make peace on one condition: that the right eye of every citizen should be put out. The people were appalled. They wept and wailed, but not one of them could think of a way to avoid this cruel punishment.

Toward evening Saul came in from the fields, driving a herd of oxen before him. He was astonished to find the entire population in a state of terror. "What is the matter?" he asked. "What has happened?"

When he heard what the enemy was threatening to do, Saul was full of anger. Immediately he summoned his army together. He sent messengers to the people of Jabesh, promising that the very next day, by the time the sun was at its highest, they would be safe. The Israelites attacked the Ammonites early the next morning. By midday they had either slain

Samuel reproaches Saul for lighting the
sacrificial fire himself

or put to flight every one of them. Saul and his people
were overjoyed, and celebrated their victory with
sacrifices to the Lord.

Two years after Saul had become king, the Philistines
gathered on the Israelites' border in enormous numbers,
preparing for invasion. Samuel told Saul to wait for seven
days, at the end of which he would come and make the burnt offering
before the battle. But at the end of seven days, there was no sign of
Samuel, and Saul grew impatient. He decided to wait no longer, but
to light the fire himself.

Suddenly he found Samuel by his side. "Why have you disobeyed
me?" Samuel asked.

"Because you did not come, and my men were scattered. The
Philistines may attack at any moment. I was afraid that if I did not
make a burnt offering to the Lord, we would be defeated."

"You have done wrong to disregard God's commandment," Samuel
reproached him. "If you had obeyed God's word, you would have been
the founder of a great kingdom. But because you went against his
word, your sons will now never succeed you: another family, not
yours, will rule Israel."

CANAANITE ALTAR
The Israelites were not
the only people to
sacrifice animals on
altars – it was a common
practice in the ancient
Middle East. The
Canaanites made
sacrifices to their gods on
rectangular – or oval –
shaped altars. These were
made of uncut field
stones, like the one
above. Canaanite altars
were usually built on
"high places" – hilltop
sites dedicated to the
worship of the gods.

God Chooses David

GOD SPOKE TO SAMUEL, telling him to go to Bethlehem where he would find a man called Jesse. "I have chosen one of the sons of Jesse to be the next king," he said.

In Bethlehem, the news of Samuel's arrival made the people tremble, for he was now a great and powerful man. But Samuel

Jesse

*Jesse's youngest son, David,
watches over the sheep*

Samuel

Samuel blesses seven of Jesse's sons, but knows that none of them has been chosen by God

reassured them. "I come in peace, to bless you and pray with you."

One by one, seven of Jesse's sons came to the prophet to be blessed. When Samuel saw the men standing before him, tall and handsome, he thought to himself, "Surely, one of these must be the chosen one." But as each of the brothers came before him in turn, he heard the Lord's voice, "This is not the man. God does not judge in the way people do. Do not look at the face but into the heart."

Finally, Samuel turned to Jesse and said, "God has chosen none of these men. Are all your children here?"

"All but the youngest, David, and he is out in the fields looking after the sheep."

"Fetch him," said Samuel.

The boy, fresh-faced and strongly built, came running in. "This is he," said God. Then Samuel took the holy oil and anointed David in front of his whole family. And from that day on the spirit of the Lord was with him.

SHEPHERD BOY
David was the youngest, and therefore the least important, of Jesse's sons. He looked after his father's sheep in the hills around Bethlehem. Out in all kinds of weather, his life would have been a lonely one as he led his sheep to good pasture, and protected them from harm. One story in the Bible tells how David risked his life by killing a bear and a lion that threatened the sheep.

Samuel anoints David the next king of the Israelites

David and Goliath

Saul's army gathers to do battle against the Philistines

David hurls a stone from his sling

SLINGSHOT
As a shepherd, David would have carried a sling for hurling stones at animals that threatened his sheep. The shepherd placed a stone in his pad, held the two ends of the sling, then swung it around at high speed. When he let go of one end, the stone would fly toward its target. Also used by soldiers, the sling was a deadly weapon.

THE PHILISTINES WERE READY for battle. On two hilltops, with only a narrow valley between, the armies were assembled, the Philistines on one, Saul and the Israelites on the other.

All of a sudden a giant man came striding down toward the valley from the Philistine camp. Goliath of Gath towered above everyone; on his head was a massive bronze helmet; he wore a breastplate of bronze, and his legs and arms were sheathed in bronze. In one hand he carried a bronze dagger, in the other an iron-headed spear as big as a tree.

"I challenge you, Saul!" bellowed Goliath. "I challenge you to send one of your men to fight me! Let the two of us decide the outcome of the war!"

At these words, Saul trembled, and the Israelites were filled with fear.

Three of Jesse's sons were among Saul's soldiers, and their brother David had left his sheep to bring them food. As he reached the camp, he heard Goliath's boastful challenge, and saw that no one dared answer it.

"I will fight the giant," he said to Saul.

"But you are only a boy. Goliath is a famous man of war."

Eventually, however, Saul was persuaded. Refusing both weapons and armor, David went to a nearby stream and picked out five smooth pebbles, which he put in his shepherd's pouch. Then, with his sling in

The stone strikes Goliath in the middle of his forehead, and kills him

Philistine army

DAVID PUT HIS HAND IN HIS BAG, AND TOOK THENCE A STONE, AND SLANG IT, AND SMOTE THE PHILISTINE IN HIS FOREHEAD.

I SAMUEL 17:49

one hand, his staff in the other, he walked toward Goliath.

"Get out of my way, boy!" the champion shouted, his voice heavy with contempt. "I do not fight with children!"

"You come to me with a dagger and a spear, but I come to you with God on my side," said David. He put down his staff, and placed a pebble in his sling. Whirling it around once, he let it fly. The stone struck Goliath in the middle of his forehead, and the giant crashed to the ground, dead.

When the Philistines saw their great champion dead, they turned and ran, leaving the Israelites to celebrate their victory.

PHILISTINE HEAD
The Philistines were one of the "Sea Peoples" who originally came from the islands in the Aegean Sea. They buried their dead in clay coffins, or sarcophagi. Strange-looking human features were engraved on the head ends of the coffins.

Saul Turns Against David

HARP
David's harp may have looked like this Jewish harp, called a *nebel*. It is made out of animal skin stretched over a rounded box. Or, David may have played a *kinnor*, a small, stringed instrument with a wooden frame.

S O DELIGHTED WAS SAUL with David's magnificent victory, that he gave him a high command in the army, and the young man came to live in Saul's own house. There David was made welcome by Saul's son, Jonathan, whom he quickly came to love as a brother. Jonathan spoke so highly of David to his father that Saul, too, soon came to look on him as a member of his own family. After a while, Saul gave his daughter, Michal, to David as a wife. Michal, a scholar, had long been in love with David, and so the match was a happy one.

To the people of Israel David was a hero. As he walked through the streets he was cheered and applauded, songs were sung and stories recounted about his defeat of Goliath. Women with tambourines danced joyfully in front of him, chanting, "Saul has slain thousands, but David has slain tens of thousands!"

Saul tries to kill David

*David dodges
Saul's spear*

Saul listened to their words, and he began to grow jealous. "If the people think so much more of him than of me," he said to himself, "he will soon be in possession of my kingdom." From that moment he began to brood, and to watch David closely.

One day David was playing his harp while Saul listened. In Saul's hand was the spear which always hung from his belt. Suddenly overcome by a passionate surge of hatred, Saul threw the spear at the young man's head. David dodged the blade, but realizing his life was now in danger, left Saul as soon as he could and went into hiding. He went first to Michal, but she quickly convinced him it was not safe to stay. She lowered him on a rope from the window, and from there he disappeared into the darkness and made his escape.

That night soldiers sent by Saul appeared at David's house demanding to see him. "He is ill in bed," said his wife. Pushing her to one side, the men burst into David's room where they saw what appeared to be a man asleep. But it was only a statue covered in goat's hair which Michal had placed under the covers to deceive them.

So David made his escape. But Saul thought only of his hatred, and how to bring about the young man's death.

Michal helps David to escape through a window

So Michal let David down through a window: and he went, and fled, and escaped.
I Samuel 19:12

Michal places a goat's hair rug under the covers, so the soldiers think it is David

David the Outlaw

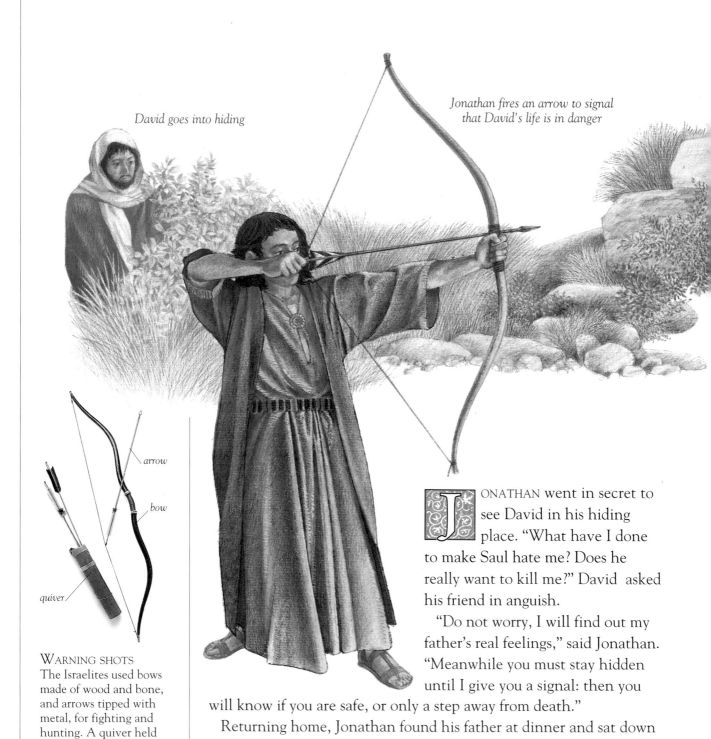

David goes into hiding

Jonathan fires an arrow to signal that David's life is in danger

arrow

bow

quiver

WARNING SHOTS
The Israelites used bows
made of wood and bone,
and arrows tipped with
metal, for fighting and
hunting. A quiver held
up to 30 arrows.

JONATHAN went in secret to
see David in his hiding
place. "What have I done
to make Saul hate me? Does he
really want to kill me?" David asked
his friend in anguish.

"Do not worry, I will find out my
father's real feelings," said Jonathan.
"Meanwhile you must stay hidden
until I give you a signal: then you
will know if you are safe, or only a step away from death."

Returning home, Jonathan found his father at dinner and sat down
opposite him. "Where is David?" the king demanded.

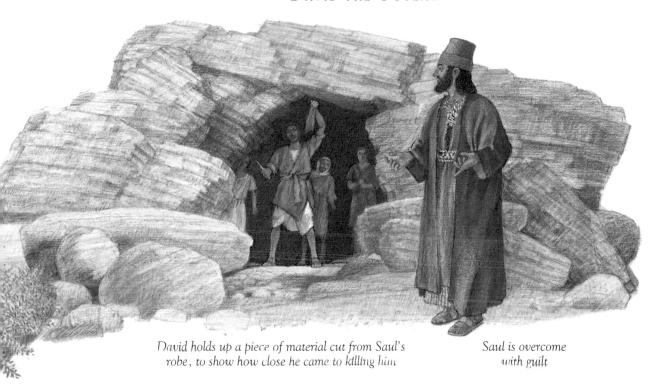

*David holds up a piece of material cut from Saul's
robe, to show how close he came to killing him*

*Saul is overcome
with guilt*

"He has gone to visit his family in Bethlehem. Believe me, Father, he has done you no harm," said Jonathan.

His face crimson with rage, Saul staggered to his feet, grabbed a spear, and flung it drunkenly at his son. "How dare you take sides against me. Bring David to me now, for he must die!" he shouted.

The next morning, as arranged, Jonathan went into the meadow where David was hiding. He fired an arrow to fall far beyond where his friend lay concealed. This signaled that David's life was in danger. The two men embraced sadly. Then they parted, Jonathan to go back to the city, David to go into the wilderness, where he was joined by a band of loyal followers.

Saul set out with his men to look for David in the desert land around En Gedi. The day was hot, and he retired into a cave – the same cave in which David and his men were hiding. Quietly David crept up behind Saul and cut off a piece of his coat. Once Saul had left the cave, David called out, "My lord king, it is I, David. See how close I came to killing you, and yet I spared your life! I would not harm someone who has been anointed by God."

At these words, Saul was overcome with guilt. "David, I have treated you badly, but you are a much greater man than I. May God be with you, and long may you reign as the future king of Israel!"

HIDEOUT
In the rugged hills and valleys around En Gedi, by the Dead Sea, there were plenty of natural caves where David and his followers could hide. In a cave, such as the one above, David would have had the advantage of seeing Saul and his army approaching from a distance.

David and Abigail

FTER WEEKS OF WANDERING in the desert, David and his followers came within a short distance of Carmel. This was the home of Nabal, a man famous for his enormous wealth. Having always treated Nabal well, David did not hesitate to send several of his men to ask for food. Nabal, however, received them rudely. "Who is this David?" he demanded. "Why should I give you anything?" And with that he turned the men away.

But Abigail, his wife, a kind and beautiful young woman, hearing what had happened, was distressed by her husband's meanness.

FIG CAKES
Abigail brought David cakes made of figs. This sweet, seedy fruit formed part of the Israelite diet. The figs could be eaten fresh, or dried and pressed into cakes. Figs were one of Canaan's most important crops.

Abigail loads her donkeys with provisions and takes them to David

She kneels before him and begs for his mercy

Secretly, she loaded five donkeys with provisions – wine, meat, bread, raisins, and fig cakes. Riding through a mountain ravine, Abigail met David and his loyal followers. Kneeling before David, she begged for his mercy. "My husband is much to blame for refusing you food," she said. "But I implore you not to take revenge!"

David, moved by her words, promised that he would leave Nabal unharmed.

When Abigail returned to Carmel, she found her husband holding a feast, surrounded by his friends and very drunk. So drunk was he that not until next morning was she able to tell him of her visit to David. As she spoke, Nabal's blood ran like ice in his veins. His heart failed him and became like stone, and within ten days he was dead.

Later, David asked Abigail to be his wife.

AND IT WAS SO, AS ABIGAIL RODE ON THE ASS, THAT SHE CAME DOWN BY THE COVERT ON THE HILL, AND BEHOLD, DAVID AND HIS MEN CAME DOWN AGAINST HER; AND SHE MET THEM.
I SAMUEL 25:20

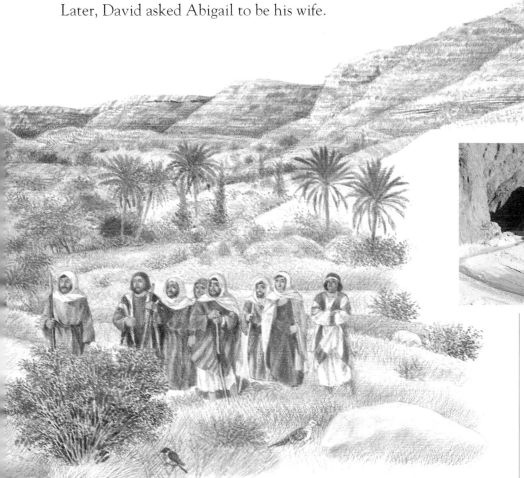

WADI
Abigail met David in a mountain ravine near Carmel. A ravine, or wadi, is formed by a stream that floods during the rainy season, but remains dry for the rest of the year. When dry, wadis were used as roadways. Wadis are common in the desert regions of the Middle East.

David's loyal followers watch close by

The Death of Saul

The witch of Endor summons the spirit of Samuel from the dead

The spirit tells Saul he will be defeated by the Philistines

Saul realizes that the voice of the spirit is indeed Samuel's

SHEOL
The Israelites saw the world as a flat disk surrounded by seas and resting on pillars. Deep in the depths of the earth was Sheol, the resting place of the dead. Saul would have believed that Samuel's spirit was called up from Sheol.

AMUEL WAS DEAD, and the whole country mourned for him, for he had been much loved. The Philistines were ready yet again for war, and yet again the Israelites were preparing to defend themselves. When Saul realized the power and size of the enemy, his heart was filled with a deadly fear. He prayed to God, but only silence answered his prayers.

Then in his misery he remembered hearing talk of a witch at Endor. Carefully disguising himself and attended by two of his men, he went by night to see her. "Ask the spirits what is to happen to me," he begged. Knowing that witchcraft was against the law, the woman was nervous, and at first refused. But Saul reassured her.

"Whom do you wish me to call up?" she asked him.

"Samuel."

No sooner had he spoken than the witch cried out in alarm.

"What do you see?" asked Saul.

"I see an old man covered in a cloak," she said. At once Saul knew that it was indeed Samuel whom she had called up from the dead.

"God has left you," said the voice of Samuel. "Tomorrow the Philistines will be victorious in battle, and you and your sons shall be slain."

The next day the Philistine army in their thousands fell upon the Israelites, who were swiftly and bloodily defeated. Hundreds were slaughtered, hundreds more ran for their lives. Jonathan and his brothers were killed. Saul, already mortally wounded, turned to his armor bearer. "Kill me!" he commanded.

But the man was afraid: he could not bring himself to kill his king. "My lord, I cannot!" he said.

So Saul plunged his sword into his breast. When the armor bearer saw the king fall, he, too, turned his blade upon himself so that he might die with him.

MOUNT GILBOA
Mount Gilboa, shown above, was the setting for the horrific battle between the Israelites and the Philistines. The mountain is in northern Canaan and overlooks the valley of Jezreel.

Saul

armor bearer

Saul, mortally wounded, commands his armor bearer to kill him

Long Live the King

JERUSALEM
Above is Jerusalem, also known as the "City of David," which became the Israelites' political and religious center. On the left is the Dome of the Rock, a Muslim mosque. It now stands on the site of Solomon's temple, which David made plans for and Solomon built.

IN THE TOWN OF HEBRON all the tribes of Israel gathered to proclaim David the new king of the Israelites. David took his people to Jerusalem, a city belonging to the Jebusites – for Jerusalem was to be his capital. But the Jebusites refused to open their gates, leaving the newcomers camped outside the walls.

However, some of David's men climbed up a waterpipe, which took them deep inside the city, and from there they were able to unlock the gates. Once inside, the Israelites defeated the Jebusites and captured the city.

The Ark of the Covenant was brought to Jerusalem, escorted by a crowd of thousands, singing and playing on pipes and tambourines.

DANCING FOR JOY
The picture above shows folk dancing in modern-day Syria. When the Israelites danced, it was a way of expressing their delight in God. On entering Jerusalem, the Israelites danced to thank God for their victory and to praise him.

The people escort the Ark into Jerusalem

As they entered the gates, trumpets sounded, and David took off his royal robes and danced for joy before the Ark of the Covenant.

When the Ark arrived at the ceremonial tent, or tabernacle, which had been built to house it, David offered burnt sacrifices to the Lord. Then he blessed his people, and gave everyone cakes and wine.

Michal, David's wife, watched him from a window as he mingled freely with the crowd. "How shameful to see the king of Israel dancing with the common people!" she said scornfully.

But David replied, "Nothing I do for the honor of God is shameful: the shame lies with those who despise me for it!" Then David resolved to build a temple in honor of the Lord.

MICHAL LOOKED THROUGH A WINDOW, AND SAW KING DAVID LEAPING AND DANCING BEFORE THE LORD; AND SHE DESPISED HIM IN HER HEART.
II SAMUEL 6:16

Michal watches David with scorn

tabernacle

Ark of the Covenant

David dances before the Ark

David and Bathsheba

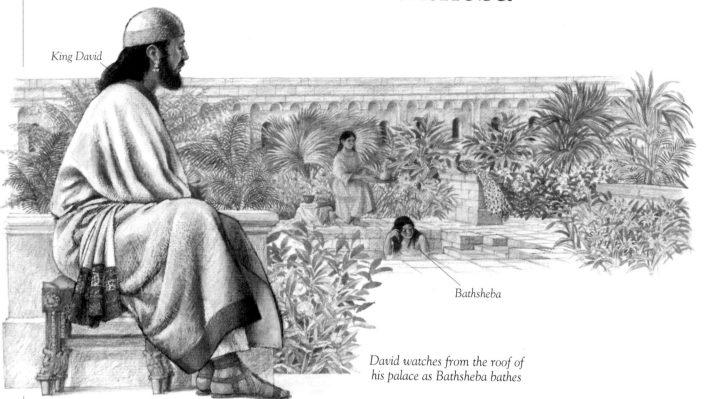

King David

Bathsheba

David watches from the roof of his palace as Bathsheba bathes

BATHING
This clay figure of a woman bathing dates from around 1000 BCE. After washing, Bathsheba would have rubbed scented oil into her skin.

ING DAVID'S ARMIES were away fighting in the field, but the king himself stayed in Jerusalem. One evening as he was sitting on the flat roof of his palace, he saw a lovely woman bathing and combing her hair. He sent a messenger to find out who she was. The answer came back that her name was Bathsheba, wife of Uriah the Hittite.

David was so struck by her beauty and grace that he gave orders for Bathsheba to be brought before him. He talked to her, courted her, and made love to her. In time she told him she was carrying his child.

Immediately David recalled her husband, Uriah, who was one of his best generals. He asked for a report on the war, and then told him to return to his own house. The next day, however, David was informed that Uriah had spent the night sleeping at the door of the palace.

"Why did you not go home and see your wife?" David asked him.

"How can I eat and drink with my wife, and sleep safe under my own roof when I know that your whole army is encamped in the

Bathsheba's husband, Uriah, is killed in battle

PET LAMB
Generally, the Israelites did not keep animals as pets, but a lamb that had lost its mother would have needed special care. A shepherd, or shepherdess, may have taken an orphaned lamb into the family home to look after it, much as the poor man cared for his ewe lamb.

open, ready to fight for the nation?" asked Uriah.

David sent Uriah back to the field with a letter to Joab, the commander of the army: "You must place Uriah in the front line, and keep him where the fighting is fiercest." Joab did as he was ordered, and during the next battle Uriah was killed.

Bathsheba grieved for her husband, but once the period of mourning was over, she agreed to marry David. After a while, she gave birth to a son.

God was displeased, and sent Nathan the prophet to show David the cruelty of his treatment of Uriah, who had been such a brave and loyal servant.

Nathan began by telling David a story. "There were two men," he said. "One was rich, with many flocks and herds, the other poor, his only possession a little ewe lamb that he loved as a daughter and fed from his own plate. A traveler arrived at the rich man's house asking to be fed. The rich man, not wishing to lose one of his own sheep, instead killed the poor man's little lamb, roasted it, and fed it to his guest."

David was shocked by Nathan's story. "The rich man should be punished!" he shouted angrily.

"But you are like the rich man," said Nathan. "And it is you who must be punished. You have sinned against God, and for this your son will die!"

THE POOR MAN HAD NOTHING, SAVE ONE LITTLE EWE LAMB, WHICH HE HAD BOUGHT AND NOURISHED UP; AND IT GREW UP TOGETHER WITH HIM, AND WITH HIS CHILDREN.
II SAMUEL 12:3

The poor man feeds his ewe lamb with his own food

Absalom's Rebellion

Absalom and his men rebel against David, but are defeated in battle

Absalom

Absalom waits at the city gate and talks to anyone who comes to see the king

Absalom makes himself popular with the people

HAIR
In Canaan, both men and women often wore their hair long and groomed. This carving shows an Assyrian official with long hair that has been carefully curled. Absalom cut his hair with a razor once a year.

S NATHAN had predicted Bathsheba's son died, but later she gave birth to another boy, who was called Solomon. God loved Solomon, but King David had many other children by many different wives, and most of them squabbled with each other. One, called Absalom, quarreled with and killed his half brother. He was then forced to flee and go into hiding. Eventually, however, David relented and allowed Absalom to return to Jerusalem.

Absalom was a young man of exceptional beauty, particularly proud of his long, thick hair. He was also ambitious, secretly determined that he should be the next king of Israel. He bought a chariot and horses and every morning he would stand at the city gate and talk to anyone who came to see the king.

Having made himself popular with the people, Absalom went to Hebron. There he raised a powerful army, with which he challenged his father to battle for the kingship.

But David rode out of Jerusalem at the head of many thousand men. As he gave his instructions to his captains, he said, "Be gentle with Absalom, for my sake."

After a long battle, the rebels were put to flight. Absalom himself escaped on the back of a mule, which, frightened by the noise of fighting, bolted into the shelter of a forest. As it galloped through the trees, Absalom's long hair was caught in the branches of an oak, and he was left dangling helplessly.

There he was found by one of David's men, who went to tell Joab, the commander of the king's army. "You have seen Absalom!" Joab exclaimed. "Why did you not kill him on the spot? I personally would have given you a handsome reward!"

"I would not have accepted it," said the soldier. "I will not lift a finger against him, for King David asked us to deal gently with his son."

Enraged, Joab grabbed three heavy spears.

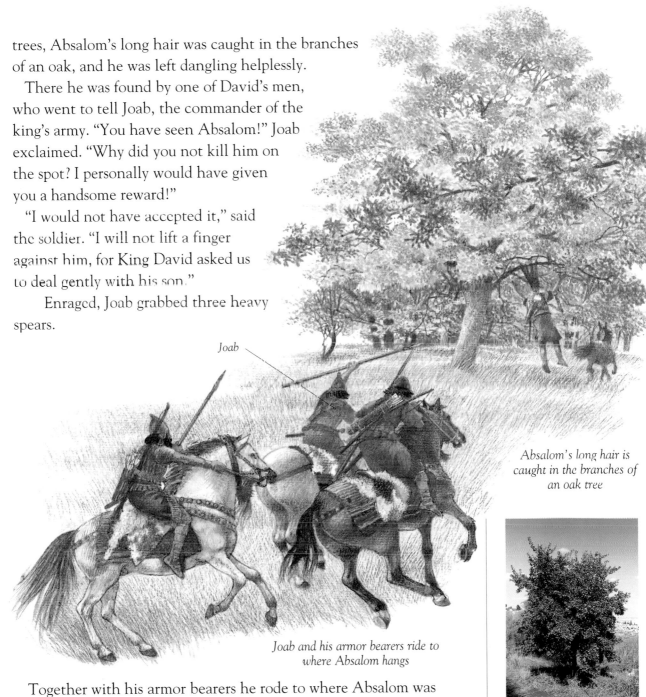

Joab

Absalom's long hair is caught in the branches of an oak tree

Joab and his armor bearers ride to where Absalom hangs

Together with his armor bearers he rode to where Absalom was hanging, a prisoner in the branches of the tree, and drove the spears into his chest. Then he gave orders for Absalom's body to be flung into a pit in the depths of the forest and covered with stones.

When David heard the news of Absalom's death, he was overcome with grief. "My son, oh my son!" he wept. "If only I had died instead of you!"

OAK TREE
The kermes oak, above, was one of several species of oak tree that grew in Canaan in ancient times. Oak trees are still found in the Middle East today.

King Solomon's Wisdom

AND THE KING SAID, "BRING ME A SWORD." AND THEY BROUGHT A SWORD BEFORE THE KING. AND THE KING SAID, "DIVIDE THE LIVING CHILD IN TWO, AND GIVE HALF TO THE ONE, AND HALF TO THE OTHER."
I KINGS 3:24-25

Solomon orders that the baby be cut in two

One woman agrees with the order

The other woman pleads for her baby's life

WHEN DAVID WAS DYING, he summoned his son, Solomon. "Soon I shall no longer be here to advise you," he said. "Always be strong and true, and always obey the word of God. If you do that, the Lord will be with you."

After David died, Solomon in his turn became king of Israel, and married the daughter of Pharaoh, king of Egypt, with whom he had made a treaty.

One night God appeared to him in a dream. "Ask for what you most want, and I will give it to you."

"You have made me king of a great people," Solomon replied. "But I have no more idea of how to govern than a child. Lord, give me wisdom."

Pleased with this answer, God said, "Because you asked nothing for yourself, neither for long life, nor wealth, nor victory over your enemies, I will grant your wish. If you do right and obey my laws, I will give you a wise and understanding heart, and you shall become known as a good king."

Soon afterward two women came before Solomon. They shared a house, and each had recently given birth to a child, but one child had died, and now both mothers were claiming the living baby as theirs.

"It is her baby who died," the first woman insisted. "Do you think I do not know my own child!"

"No, no!" cried the other. "It is her baby who is dead: in the night while I slept, she stole mine from my side!"

"Bring me my sword," said Solomon. The sword was brought. "Cut the child in two, and give half to each of the women standing here."

"Yes, O wise King, let neither of us have him," said one. "Cut him in two!"

But the other woman burst into tears and wrung her hands. "Do not kill my baby!" she cried. "I would rather give him away than have him hurt!" By this Solomon knew that she was the true mother, and he gave the child to her.

When the people heard of the judgment of Solomon they looked at their king with new respect, for they knew such wisdom could come to him only from God.

KING SOLOMON
Solomon was renowned for his wisdom, and this is shown in the story of the two women: he knew that the real mother would not agree to her baby being killed. The king wrote many wise sayings: most of the Book of Proverbs is thought to have been written by him. Under Solomon's rule the Israelites entered a golden age of peace and prosperity. This was crowned by the building of the temple, named after him, in Jerusalem.

The baby is given to the true mother

Solomon's Temple

CEDARS OF LEBANON
Large, evergreen cedar trees covered the hills of Lebanon in Solomon's time. Cedarwood was valued for its beauty, fragrance, and strength.

N OW THAT THERE WAS peace at last, Solomon's greatest wish was to carry out the plan of his father, David, to build a temple for the worship of God. He sent word to Hiram, king of Tyre, asking him for wood from the great cedars of Lebanon. The huge trees were felled, then roped to rafts and floated down the coast. At the same time thousands of laborers quarried and cut the stones for the foundations and outer walls of the temple.

It took four years to lay the foundations, and three to build the temple upon them. Inside the temple, the walls were of cedarwood, carved with flowers and trees and painted with gold. The altar, too, was covered in gold.

When it was finished, Solomon, accompanied by the priests and tribal leaders, brought the Ark of the Covenant to the temple, where it was placed carefully in the inner sanctuary.

Suddenly the temple was filled with a cloud, so the priests could not carry out their duties. It was the glory of God filling the house of the Lord.

Laborers cut the stones for the temple

SOLOMON'S TEMPLE
Solomon's temple replaced the tabernacle, or sacred tent, in providing a permanent home for the Ark of the Covenant. The Ark, flanked by two golden cherubim, was placed in the innermost room, the Holy of Holies. The temple was at the center of the Israelites' faith because it was the place where God was (see page 17).

It takes seven years to build Solomon's temple

Winged cherubim are carved for the inside of the temple

CARVED IVORY Cherubim, winged creatures, were carved on the inside of the temple. They may have looked like this sphinx from Nimrud in Assyria.

The Queen of Sheba

THE QUEEN OF SHEBA had heard about the wisdom of Solomon, and she wished to see for herself if all she had heard was true. So she traveled a long way from the distant land of Sheba with a great camel caravan, loaded with spices and gold and precious stones, until she came to Jerusalem. The king received her courteously, and she asked him many

The queen of Sheba travels to Jerusalem

She is accompanied by a great camel caravan, loaded with spices and gold and precious stones

THE QUEEN'S JOURNEY
Sheba was probably in southwest Arabia. The queen of Sheba traveled about 1,000 miles (1,600 km) to visit Solomon. On the way, she would have taken the King's Highway, a major international trade route that was controlled by Israel during the reigns of David and Solomon.

difficult questions. But none was too difficult for Solomon: he answered them all.

Then she looked around her, at his servants and his ministers, at his magnificent golden palace and happy, prosperous people, and she knew that here was a man both wise and good. "I would not believe it, until I had seen with my own eyes," she said. "Israel is fortunate in its king."

She gave Solomon many magnificent gifts, while he in his turn presented her with everything her heart desired. His wealth and generosity were without limit, and the queen returned to her own country laden with the riches of Israel.

King Solomon comes out from his palace to receive the queen

PRECIOUS GIFTS
Sheba became a wealthy land by trading spices, gold, and jewels. When the queen of Sheba visited King Solomon and brought expensive gifts with her, she may have wished to make a trade agreement with the king.

AFRICAN QUEEN
Legend has it that the queen of Sheba ruled over Ethiopia and Egypt.

Elijah in the Wilderness

AFTER THE DEATH of Solomon, his son Rehoboam became king. There was unrest among the tribes in the north, but Rehoboam did not listen to the people's troubles. The tribes rebelled and the kingdom was split in two, into Israel and Judah. Then, the people of Israel turned against God. The times were so wicked that the prophet Elijah foretold there would be a drought lasting many years.

The Lord spoke to Elijah. "Go to the stream that runs in the valley of Kerith, and live there in secret. You can drink from the brook, and the ravens will bring you food." And indeed every morning and evening ravens appeared with bread and meat in their beaks; but soon the stream dried up from the lack of rain.

In obedience to God, Elijah then went to the city of Sidon, where he met a woman gathering sticks

TWO KINGDOMS
Solomon, who belonged to the tribe of Judah, had not always treated the northern tribes well. When Rehoboam became king these tribes rebelled. The kingdom was then split into two: Israel, with Samaria as its capital, in the north; Judah, with Jerusalem as its capital, in the south.

Elijah drinks from the brook and is fed by ravens

*Elijah brings the woman's
son back to life*

outside the city walls. "Please, give me something to eat," Elijah
asked her.

"I have nothing but a jar of flour and a little oil," she said. "And
with that I must feed myself and my son, or we will starve."

"Go to your house, and there you will find enough flour and enough
oil to last until the rains come." And it happened just as the prophet
said. There was food every day for the woman, her son, and for Elijah.

But then the woman's son fell ill and died. "Do you call yourself a
man of God!" she cried to Elijah. "You, who have let God take my
son from me!" Elijah gently lifted up the boy, laid him on his own
bed, and three times he bent over him.

"O Lord," he prayed. "Let this child's life return." And in a short
while the boy took a deep breath, opened his eyes, and sat up. Elijah
lifted the child and brought him to his mother, who was overjoyed.
"Now I know you are truly a man of God," she said.

RAVENS
According to Old
Testament law, a raven
was unclean and could
not be sacrificed or eaten.
In spite of this, God sent
ravens to bring food to
Elijah in the desert,
showing that the most
humble can serve God.

The Israelites Turn Against God

BAAL
This bronze idol from about 1400-1300 BCE probably represents Baal, the chief Canaanite god. The Israelites may have begun to worship Baal because he was supposed to control rainfall, which the Israelites depended on for survival.

THE DROUGHT HAD LASTED FOR THREE YEARS when Elijah the prophet went to Samaria to see Ahab, king of Israel, who had become a follower of the god Baal. He told Ahab to summon the children of Israel and all the priests, and bring them together on Mount Carmel. There Elijah said to them, "You cannot worship both Baal and God!" But the people remained silent. He told them to build an altar to Baal while he built an altar to God. They laid wood and a sacrificial calf on each of the altars. "Let the true God set alight the altar fire!" cried Elijah.

The priests of Baal lifted up their arms and called on their god to send them fire. "O, Baal, hear us!" they shouted. But the hours passed and nothing happened, and the fire remained unlit.

"Perhaps he sleeps!" mocked Elijah. He gave orders for barrels of

Elijah builds an altar to God, and it roars into flames

The priests build an altar to Baal, but it remains unlit

water to be emptied over his altar, so that the wood was soaked and impossible to burn. He spoke quietly to God. "Lord God of Israel, I ask you to send fire so that the hearts of your people may return to you."

"THERE ARISETH A LITTLE CLOUD OUT OF THE SEA, LIKE A MAN'S HAND."
I KINGS 18:44

Elijah

servant

A little cloud appears, no bigger than a man's hand

Elijah tells his servant to let Ahab know that the rains have come

Instantly the pile of sodden logs roared into flames, and within seconds the calf, the wood, and the stones on which they lay were burnt to blackened ashes. At this, the people fell on their faces and honored God.

Then Elijah went to the summit of Carmel and told his servant to look out to sea. "There is nothing," said the young man, "only a clear sky and a calm sea." Elijah told him to look again. "Still I see nothing." Seven times he looked, and after the seventh time he turned to the prophet saying, "Still I see nothing – nothing but a little cloud, no bigger than a man's hand."

"Go quickly to Ahab, and tell him that the rains have come!" Almost before Elijah had spoken, the sky grew black, and the rain came lashing down, and a great wind arose that drove the water inward over the whole country. Ahab rode off to the town of Jezreel, but Elijah, tucking his cloak into his belt, ran ahead of Ahab.

MOUNT CARMEL
Carmel is the name of a mountain range which extends from the edge of the Jezreel Valley to the Mediterranean Sea. It reaches a height of about 1,750 ft (535 m). In biblical times it was covered in oak trees, olive groves, and vineyards, and it is still rich in vegetation today.

Naboth's Vineyard

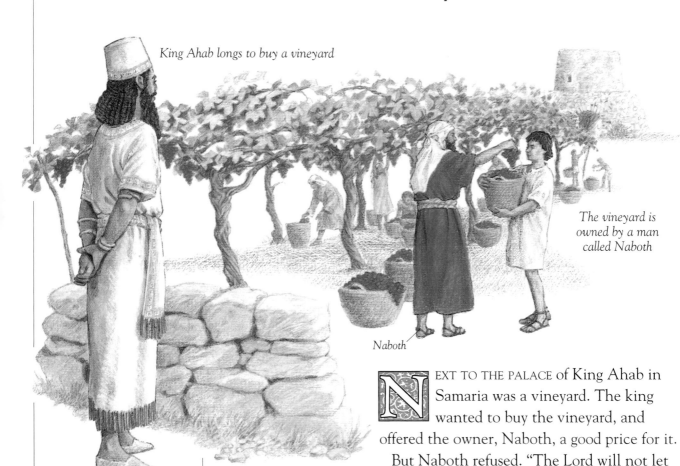

King Ahab longs to buy a vineyard

The vineyard is owned by a man called Naboth

Naboth

VINEYARD
This Assyrian carving shows a king and queen in a vineyard. The vines are trained and lifted off the ground by supports.

NEXT TO THE PALACE of King Ahab in Samaria was a vineyard. The king wanted to buy the vineyard, and offered the owner, Naboth, a good price for it. But Naboth refused. "The Lord will not let me part with my inheritance," he told the king.

Ahab, who was used to being obeyed, was enraged. He flung himself down on his bed, turned his face to the wall, and refused both food and drink. His wife, Jezebel, was worried. "Please tell me what is troubling you," she begged him. But when she heard what the matter was, she laughed. "Now you may eat and drink with a light heart! I will see that you get your vineyard – in fact it is as good as yours already."

Jezebel wrote to all the officials and noblemen of the city, signing the letters with Ahab's name, and sealing them with the royal seal. In them she gave instructions that a day of fasting should be held. Naboth was to be set up in a position of great importance. Two men were to sit opposite him and accuse him of speaking against God, a crime that carried a sentence of death.

Everything happened as Jezebel had planned. Naboth was accused, seized, taken outside the city walls, and stoned to death. "Now the vineyard is yours," said Jezebel in triumph to her husband.

Ahab lost no time in going to the vineyard, anxious to inspect his new property. But he found he was not alone. God had spoken to the prophet, Elijah, and sent him to rebuke the king. "This vineyard has been bought with the death of an innocent man!" thundered Elijah. "And just as the dogs lick his blood from the roadside, so will they lick yours. For your death, and that of Jezebel, will be as cruel and violent as Naboth's!"

Ahab was appalled when he heard the prophet's words and was overcome with shame. He tore his clothes, dressed himself in sackcloth to show his remorse, refused to eat, and fell into deep despair.

When God saw that Ahab was truly sorry for what he had done, the Lord spoke again to Elijah. "Because this man has seen the error of his ways, I will be merciful to him. He may live out his days in peace, but because of the serious wrong done, there will come a time when disaster will fall upon his descendants."

Jezebel

Naboth is seized by soldiers and taken outside to be stoned, as Jezebel looks on

King Ahab takes possession of Naboth's vineyard

Elijah rebukes him for killing Naboth

Ahab is overcome with shame and dresses in sackcloth

Elijah's Final Journey

Elisha

Elijah beats the surface of the River Jordan with his cloak and the waters divide

ONE DAY ELIJAH WAS TRAVELING WITH ELISHA, whom he had chosen to be his successor. Elijah, knowing that he was soon to die, asked Elisha to go with him no farther. Elisha loved the older man, and wanted to stay with him. "I shall not leave you," he said. So the two men continued on their way.

At Bethel, Elijah again turned to Elisha. "You must stay here, while I go on alone." But still Elisha would not leave him.

Finally, they came to the River Jordan. Elijah took off his cloak and beat the surface of the water with it. The waters divided, and the prophets crossed the river, walking on a pathway of dry land.

Suddenly a chariot of fire appeared out of the sky, drawn by horses flaming scarlet and gold. Before Elisha knew what was happening, Elijah was whirled up into the chariot, which, with the sound of a shrieking, rushing wind, disappeared from sight. Elisha, staring up into the clouds, cried out in wonder. But Elijah was never seen again.

Slowly Elisha took up Elijah's cloak and hit the surface of the river, calling on God to help him. The waters parted and he walked to the other side on dry land. The spirit of Elijah was now with him.

CHARIOT OF GOLD
Above is a gold model of a chariot pulled by four horses. It dates from around 500 BCE. In ancient times, chariots were used in warfare and in ceremonies. In battle, a chariot usually carried two men: a driver who held the reins; and a warrior who carried a bow and arrow or a spear.

Elijah is whirled up into the skies in a chariot of fire

Elisha takes up Elijah's cloak

Elisha and the Woman of Shunem

N HIS TRAVELS ELISHA often visited the city of Shunem. In the city lived a rich woman who invited him to eat with her and her husband every time he passed by. The woman said that Elisha could stay whenever he wished, and made ready a little room for him on the roof, with a bed, a table, a stool, and a lamp.

One evening as Elisha lay on his bed, he called his servant, Gehazi. "How can I repay the kindness of this woman?" he asked.

"I know that what she wants most is a child," Gehazi replied. "But her husband is too old to father children."

"Ask her to come here," said Elisha. The woman came, and stood in the doorway to hear what Elisha had to say.

"Soon," he told her, "you will have a son."

"No, that cannot be," she protested. But just as the prophet said, within a year she gave birth to a boy.

ELISHA
The painting above is of the prophet Elisha. When Elisha took up Elijah's cloak, it symbolized that he was chosen by God to succeed Elijah as the prophet of Israel. In the Bible, Elisha is described as being bald-headed, and once he was mocked by some children for his baldness. Two bears then appeared and attacked the children.

The woman listens as Elisha tells her she will have a son

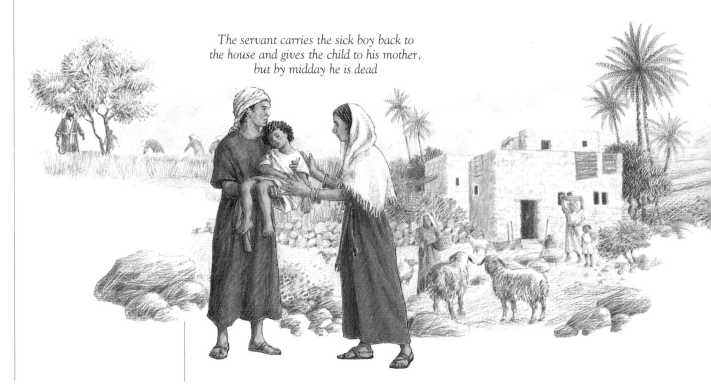

The servant carries the sick boy back to the house and gives the child to his mother, but by midday he is dead

SHUNEM
The town of Shunem, present day Solem, lies in the fertile Jezreel Valley. The town is about 3 miles (5 km) north of the town of Jezreel, near Mount Gilboa. Shunem was situated on a well-used route, which explains why Elisha often visited the town.

When the boy was older, he went out one morning to find his father who was harvesting in the fields. "Father, help me! There is a pain in my head which I cannot bear!" Frightened by his son's appearance, his father told a servant to carry him at once to the house. There his mother took him and held him on her lap, but by midday he was dead. With tears running down her cheeks, she carried the lifeless body to Elisha's room, laid it on the bed, and closed the door.

"Quickly!" she said to her husband. "Fetch a donkey, and let me have a servant to accompany me. I am going to find Elisha."

Traveling as fast as they could, they soon caught up with the prophet at Mount Carmel. Dismounting, the woman clutched Elisha's feet, but Gehazi pushed her away. "Leave her alone," Elisha said. "She is in distress, and I must know what is wrong." As soon as the woman had spoken, Elisha said to Gehazi, "Take my staff and, girding your loins, run as fast as you can to Shunem. Go to the boy, and touch his face with the staff. I and the boy's mother will follow you."

Gehazi did as his master had said. On entering the house, he touched the boy's face with the staff, but the body remained still and cold. "The boy is dead," he whispered sadly as Elisha arrived. Elisha went alone to the room in which the body lay. Closing the door behind him, he knelt and prayed to God. Then very carefully he lay down on top of the child, putting his mouth to the boy's mouth, his eyes against his eyes, his hands against the dead boy's hands. As he did so he felt the flesh beneath him grow warm. Elisha stood up and watched as the color returned to the face of what only minutes ago had been a lifeless body.

After the boy's mother has found Elisha, they travel back to Shunem together

Elisha's servant, Gehazi, runs on ahead with Elisha's staff in his hand

Suddenly the boy sneezed, and sneezed again. Then he opened his eyes and sat up.

"Come and embrace your son!" Elisha called. The woman ran into the room and gasped. Falling on her knees before the prophet, she thanked him with all her heart. Then, hand in hand, she and her son left the room together.

GIRDED LOINS
Gehazi "girded his loins" when he ran to Shunem. This means that he would have put his robe between his legs and tucked it into his belt, like the Syrian workman shown in the picture. Laborers often did this to give them greater freedom of movement when they were working.

ELISHA WENT UP, AND LAY UPON THE CHILD, AND PUT HIS MOUTH UPON HIS MOUTH, AND HIS EYES UPON HIS EYES, AND HIS HANDS UPON HIS HANDS: AND HE STRETCHED HIMSELF UPON THE CHILD; AND THE FLESH OF THE CHILD WAXED WARM.
II KINGS 4:34

Elisha brings the boy back to life

Elisha and Naaman

king of Israel

Naaman presents a letter to the king of Israel, asking to be cured of his leprosy

Naaman

NAAMAN, THE COMMANDER OF THE SYRIAN ARMY, was a brave and clever soldier, but for some years he had suffered from the skin disease of leprosy. Naaman's wife had recently taken as a maid a young Israelite who had been captured in battle.

SYRIAN KING
This ivory figure of a Syrian king is thought to be Hazael, who fought against the Israelites around the time of Elisha.

The girl said to her mistress, "How I wish my master could go to the prophet Elisha, who is in Samaria, for I know he could cure him!"

This was repeated to Naaman, who went at once to the king of Syria. "Of course you must go," said the king. "I myself will write a letter on your behalf to the king of Israel, asking that your leprosy be treated." And so Naaman set off, taking with him the letter and a splendid collection of gifts: ten talents of silver, six thousand pieces of gold, and ten complete sets of richly embroidered clothing.

When Naaman presented the king of Syria's letter, the king of Israel was angry. "Am I expected to work miracles?" he demanded. "This is only an excuse for Syria to quarrel with us yet again!"

Naaman

Naaman drives up to
Elisha's door in his chariot

Elisha's messenger tells
Naaman to go and
bathe seven times in the
River Jordan

RIVER JORDAN
The River Jordan was the
longest and most
important river in
Canaan. "Jordan" means
"flowing downward": the
river begins at Lake
Huleh in the north and
flows down to the Sea of
Galilee. From there it
drops lower until it
reaches the Dead Sea.
The distance from the
Sea of Galilee to the
Dead Sea is 70 miles (113
km), but the river winds
so much that it is more
than twice that long.

Elisha heard what had happened and he sent word to the court. "Let
Naaman come to me," he said, "and his wish shall be granted." When
Naaman drove up to Elisha's door with his chariot and horses, Elisha
remained inside, sending a messenger in his place. "The prophet says
you must go down to the River Jordan and bathe seven times in the
water. Then you will be cured."

Naaman was outraged. "Why did Elisha himself not speak to me?
All he had to do was touch me with his hand and I would have been
healed! And why the Jordan? We have greater rivers in my own land."
In a fury he turned to leave, but one of his servants stopped him.

"Master," he said. "If the prophet had asked of you some difficult
task, you would have done it without question. But all he
requires is that you bathe in the River Jordan: should you
not agree to this simple instruction?"

Realizing the sense in the man's words, Naaman went down to
the river and immersed himself seven times in the water. When
he stepped out on the bank after the seventh time, he saw that
his skin, which had been covered in sores, was as smooth
and clean as a child's.

Overcome with joy, he returned to Elisha to thank
him. "Now I know that there is no god but the God of
Israel!" He begged Elisha to accept the magnificent
presents he had brought with him from Syria. Elisha
refused his gifts, but blessed him and sent him on his way.

Naaman is healed in the River Jordan

Conquering Nations

In THE 600 YEARS between 900 BCE and 300 BCE, the people of Israel and Judah were conquered by three powerful nations from the east: first the Assyrians, followed by the Babylonians and then the Persians.

The Assyrians

For many years the Assyrians had a powerful and very skilled army. From 750 BCE they were a constant threat to Israel and Judah.

The Bible describes the attacks of the Assyrian king, Sennacherib, on the cities of Judah. Many carved stone panels, or "reliefs," have been found in Nineveh, the Assyrian capital city, showing their army, which was well equipped with chariots, bowmen, spearmen, and siege towers.

The Assyrians recorded their history on clay tablets and cylinders. In 1853, archaeologists at Nineveh found a clay tablet describing a great flood that destroyed all life. It is similar in many ways to the story in the Bible about Noah and the ark. The version found at Nineveh is called "The

THE SIEGE OF LACHISH
The limestone relief below is a detail of the Siege of Lachish, the city that was captured by the army of the Assyrian king, Sennacherib. The story of the battle is told in the wall reliefs, which are from Sennacherib's palace at Nineveh.

Epic of Gilgamesh," because one of the main characters is Gilgamesh, a hero-king.

The Assyrians worshiped a god called Ashur, whose main temple was at Assur. The temple at Nineveh was for worship of Ishtar, the goddess of war and love. Other gods were linked to different aspects of life: Nabu with wisdom and Ninurta with hunting.

The Babylonians

Later the Assyrians became less powerful, until in 612 BCE the Babylonians captured Nineveh and began to conquer the Assyrian empire. The Babylonian king, Nebuchadnezzar, soon ruled Judah, but when that area became rebellious, he ordered the temple in Jerusalem to be destroyed.

After the destruction of the temple, many people were taken to live in exile in Babylon.

This was in 586 BCE. At the same time large numbers of people were forced to live in exile in Babylon. King Nebuchadnezzar made use of the finest craftsmen to rebuild the city of Babylon. The walls and the hanging gardens were among the Seven Wonders of the Ancient World.

The northern entrance to the city was guarded by the Ishtar Gate, which was covered in brilliant blue tiles, decorated with bulls and dragons. Two of the main buildings were a grand palace and a temple dedicated to Marduk. The temple was at the top of a ziggurat, or tower, that stood over 330 feet (around 100 m) high. Some people say that it was the building referred to in the story of the Tower of Babel.

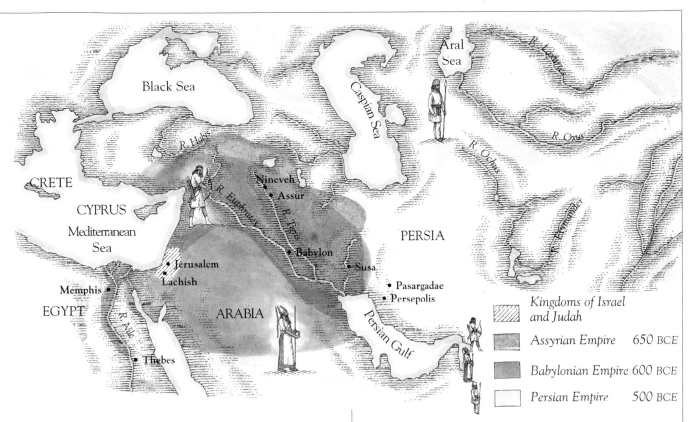

The map above shows the three nations that conquered the people of Israel between 900 BCE and 300 BCE.

In spite of the beauty of the city, many of the people who had come from Judah longed for their homeland. They wrote about weeping for Jerusalem as they sat by the River Euphrates, the "waters of Babylon." While in exile, they began to meet together and worship God in buildings which came to be known as "synagogues." But the temple in Jerusalem remained the place where they most wanted to carry out their worship.

THE GATEWAY TO BABYLON

Hanging gardens

Nebuchadnezzar's palace, built around four courtyards

Ishtar Gate, decorated with enamel bricks of bulls and dragons

Walls of the city

A brick frieze of a Persian guard.

The Persians

Babylonia's glory only lasted until 539 BCE when Cyrus the Great, king of Persia, invaded the country and attacked the capital city. He entered it by diverting the River Euphrates and marching his soldiers along the dried-up riverbed. The "Cyrus cylinder" in the British Museum records his feelings: "As I entered Babylon peacefully, and took up my seat of government in the royal palace amid rejoicing and exultation, Marduk, the great lord, inclined the hearts of the Babylonians toward me."

Cyrus controlled an empire that stretched over an area of 3,000 miles (5,000 km) and was divided into 20 provinces. He made the Persian empire richer by avoiding war, and he sent exiles back to their homelands. So, after 50 years, the people of Judah (the Jews) returned to Jerusalem.

The Prophet Isaiah

ISAIAH WAS A PROPHET of the Lord. Through him God spoke to the people. Isaiah warned them what would happen if they failed to obey God's commandments; he told them, too, of the coming of the Messiah, who would bring hope and the chance of salvation to everyone on earth.

One day in the temple in Jerusalem, Isaiah had a vision. He saw God high up on a throne. God's robes were so vast that they swirled and billowed into every corner of the temple. Above were the seraphs: each had six wings, two to cover his face, two to cover his feet, and two to fly. Continuously they sang, "Holy, holy, holy is the Lord!" And at the sound of their voices the chamber shook to its foundations and the room was filled with smoke.

"When I hear these words," Isaiah cried, "I know how unclean are the words that come from my mouth!" As he spoke he saw one of the seraphs take a red-hot coal from the altar and fly toward him. The seraph touched Isaiah's lips with the burning coal, and said, "Now your guilt is burned away and you are without sin."

Then he heard God saying, "Who can I send?"

Isaiah replied, "Here am I: send me."

"You must take my message to the people," said the Lord. "But you will find that at first they will not listen or understand, and they will refuse to be healed."

Isaiah was saddened by God's message. But throughout his life he continued to listen to the word of God. His spirits rose when he heard tell of the time to come, when happiness and joy will be everywhere. The desert will flower, the weak become strong, the lame man leap like a deer. The Lord will walk in the wilderness. God will come down to earth to tend to the people as lovingly as a shepherd tends his lambs, giving them food and water and protecting them from evil. Those who follow in the way of the Lord will be given new strength, and will be safe forever after.

Isaiah sees a vision in the temple

HE SHALL FEED HIS FLOCK LIKE A SHEPHERD: HE SHALL GATHER THE LAMBS WITH HIS ARM, AND CARRY THEM IN HIS BOSOM, AND SHALL GENTLY LEAD THOSE THAT ARE WITH YOUNG.

ISAIAH 40:11

Hezekiah's Gold

 HE KING OF ASSYRIA swept through Israel with his army, slaying all who stood in his way, burning crops, laying siege to cities, and taking prisoner anyone who did not escape.

This terrible punishment had fallen on the children of Israel because they had disobeyed the Lord. In recent years they had grown greedy and corrupt; they had ignored the warnings of the prophets, and returned to worshiping false gods. And now their country was occupied, and the ten tribes were forced to work as slaves.

In time a new king ascended the throne of Judah. Hezekiah was not only a wise ruler but a good man who obeyed God's laws. He destroyed the pagan altars and insisted that his people keep the ten commandments. A brave warrior, he had won many victories against his enemies, but not even he could withstand the might of King Sennacherib of Assyria.

Desperate to stop the invaders, Hezekiah sent word to Sennacherib, begging him to withdraw his army. "If you agree to leave my land," he said, "I will pay any price you name."

The Assyrian king demanded huge sums in silver and gold, and in order to find them the precious metals were stripped from the very walls and pillars of the temple. Sennacherib kept the treasure, but broke his promise to go, ordering his soldiers to attack Jerusalem itself. Once the city was surrounded, he sent a message demanding that Hezekiah surrender.

Not knowing where else to turn, Hezekiah went to the temple to pray and ask for help from the prophet Isaiah. "Do not be afraid," said Isaiah. "God will defend you and save the city."

That night the angel of death flew low over the Assyrian camp, leaving many hundreds of thousands dead. In the morning instead of an army, Sennacherib saw only rows and rows of bodies. Turning his back on Jerusalem, he made his way home to Nineveh.

HEZEKIAH'S TUNNEL King Hezekiah once ordered that a tunnel be dug beneath Jerusalem, so that the city's water supply would not be cut off by the invading Assyrians. Today, water still flows through Hezekiah's Tunnel.

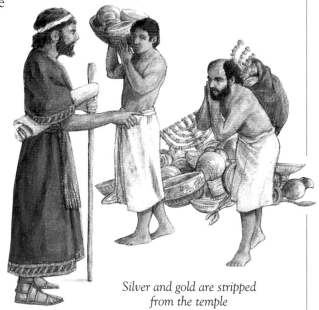

Silver and gold are stripped from the temple

Josiah and the Scroll of the Law

Josiah is only eight years old when he becomes king of Judah

OSIAH, SON OF AMON, became king of Judah when he was only eight years old. From his earliest childhood he loved God, and when he was a man he gave orders for the temple in Jerusalem, God's house, to be repaired and put in order, for it had grown shabby over the years.

While the work was carried out, the high priest discovered in a corner of the temple the scroll containing God's law, the only copy that the Israelites had. This he took to the royal scribe, Shaphan, asking him to show it to the king. When Josiah heard the scribe read from the scroll, he fell into deep despair, tearing his clothes, and weeping with sorrow. "We have forgotten God's law, and grown selfish and corrupt. How angry the Lord must be!" He told Shaphan to find out what fate was in store for his disobedient people.

Shaphan went to Jerusalem to consult Huldah, the prophetess.

"The Lord knows that the people have turned away from the law," said Huldah. "They will be punished for this, and Jerusalem will fall on hard times. But because King Josiah is a good man and has repented of the evil around him, all will be well while he lives."

ASHTORETH
This gold pendant (c1500 BCE) represents Ashtoreth, or Astarte, the Canaanite goddess of love and fertility, and the partner of the god Baal. Josiah destroyed an altar dedicated to Ashtoreth.

Repairs on the temple are carried out

The high priest discovers the scroll of the law

Josiah reads the scroll of the law to the people

All the altars and statues of false gods are smashed and burned

THE KING WENT UP INTO THE HOUSE OF THE LORD, AND ALL THE MEN OF JUDAH AND ALL THE INHABITANTS OF JERUSALEM WITH HIM, AND THE PRIESTS, AND THE PROPHETS, AND ALL THE PEOPLE, BOTH SMALL AND GREAT: AND HE READ IN THEIR EARS ALL THE WORDS OF THE BOOK OF THE COVENANT.
II KINGS 23:2

KIDRON VALLEY
The Israelites burnt their altars and statues to false gods in the Kidron Valley, on the eastern slopes of Jerusalem. Later, idols were regularly destroyed and left here. The valley is also a place of burial.

When Josiah heard this, he called his people together in the temple, and read to them the scroll of the law. He took an oath that from this day he would keep the word of God; and his people promised that they, too, would obey God's word.

Then Josiah commanded that all the altars and statues of false gods be smashed and burned. "Now my country is cleansed," he said, "and once again we may celebrate Passover." There was much rejoicing in Jerusalem that day, for the Lord was pleased by Josiah's repentance.

Jeremiah and the Potter's Wheel

ALMOND TREE
The almond was the first tree to blossom in the spring. Its nuts were used for making oil. Just as Jeremiah is watching the almond tree, God is watching the world. The Hebrew for "watching" is similar to "almond tree."

GOD SPOKE TO A YOUNG MAN called Jeremiah, telling him that he had been chosen as a prophet. "But I am young," said Jeremiah, "and know nothing!"

"Do not be afraid," said the Lord, "for I am with you." Then God's hand touched the man's mouth. "Now I have put words into your mouth. Tell me, what do you see?"

"I see the branch of an almond tree in bloom."

"Yes, you are right. I am watching to see that my word is fulfilled. What else do you see?"

"I see a boiling cauldron on the fire, tilted toward the north."

"It is from the north that disaster will come, a terrible punishment that will fall upon the land of Judah. For my people have forgotten me, and they worship false gods. You must speak to them, Jeremiah, tell them what I intend. They will turn on you, but you need fear nothing while I am with you!"

Then God sent Jeremiah to the house of a potter, who was at work at his wheel. Jeremiah watched the clay take shape; but the potter saw the shape was lopsided, and taking the wet clay in his hands, squeezed and molded it until he had made the jar perfect.

"Israel is like clay in my hands," said the Lord. "If my people persist in doing evil, they will be destroyed. But if they repent, I will make of them something good and strong. Go, Jeremiah, and tell them this."

The prophet did as God had said. He bought a clay jar; then he summoned the priests and wise men, and led them into the valley of Ben Hinnom.

"You will suffer war, famine, and plague unless you give up worshiping Baal and all your other false gods!" he told them.

In the silence that followed, Jeremiah lifted up the clay jar and hurled it to the ground so that it shattered into a thousand pieces. "Just as I have destroyed this jar, so will God

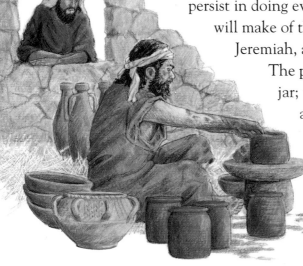
Jeremiah watches a potter shaping clay at his wheel

Jeremiah hurls a clay jar to the ground

He tells the priests and the wise men that just as he has destroyed the jar, so will God destroy the wicked Judeans

destroy the people of Judah if they do not listen to the Lord's word!"

But the Judeans did not listen, and the day soon came when Jeremiah's prophesy was fulfilled. Nebuchadnezzar, king of Babylon, sent a great army to attack Jerusalem. The city was taken and many of its people were led in chains to Babylon. Nebuchadnezzar chose a new king, Zedekiah, to rule Judah. Zedekiah had to obey the Babylonian king if Jerusalem were to be left in peace.

"Now what do you see?" the Lord asked Jeremiah.

"I see two baskets of figs set down outside the temple. One basket is full of figs that are ripe and juicy, the other full of bruised, rotten fruit that no one would want to eat."

"The Judeans in Babylon are like the ripe figs: they will repent of their sins, and I will bring them out of captivity and look after them well. But King Zedekiah and those Judeans who stayed in Jerusalem will not repent. They are rotten to the core, and nowhere shall they ever find rest or prosperity."

The ripe figs are like the repentant Judeans, while the rotten figs are like those who do not repent

ripe figs   rotten figs

POTTER
Pottery is an ancient craft. This Egyptian figure of a potter at his wheel dates from around 2500 BCE. Potters "threw" their clay pots on a wooden or stone wheel. They placed the clay on the wheel, then turned the wheel with their hand or feet as they molded the clay. God compared his control over people to the potter's control of clay.

The Israelites in Captivity

YEARS PASSED, and the prophet Jeremiah, knowing that Jerusalem was in terrible danger, tried to warn the people. "You will die if you remain here," he said. "Soon the city will be in the hands of the Babylonians, and only those who leave now will survive."

Among those listening were some army officers, and they complained bitterly about Jeremiah to Zedekiah, king of Jerusalem. "It is not for me to interfere," said Zedekiah. "You must do with him as you choose." So the officers seized the prophet, and lowered him by a rope into a deep, dark pit, whose stone floor was thickly covered in mud. There was nothing in the pit either to eat or drink.

Ebed-Melech, a member of the royal household, discovered what

Jeremiah is lowered into a pit by King Zedekiah's men

The king relents, and Jeremiah is hauled to the surface

ZODIAC SIGNS
The Babylonians are thought to have invented the signs of the zodiac. The picture above shows part of a Babylonian boundary stone, built to honor the military services of a captain of chariots called Ritti-Marduk. The man firing the bow represents the ninth sign of the zodiac, Sagittarius, the archer.

had happened, and knew that Jeremiah would die if left in captivity. He went at once to the king, who agreed to the prisoner's release.

Ebed-Melech went with thirty men to the dungeon with ropes and a pile of old rags. These he threw down to Jeremiah. "Put the ropes under your arms, and bind them with these rags so that the rope will not hurt you." Then they hauled Jeremiah slowly to the surface.

But still Jeremiah's warnings were ignored. Within a short while Nebuchadnezzar, king of Babylon, laid siege to the city. For two years the enemy army surrounded the walls, so that no one could go in or out. The people were sick and starving, and at last in despair they threw open the gates, and Nebuchadnezzar took possession of Jerusalem.

Zedekiah, meanwhile, had fled with a small group of men, but he was soon captured. His sons were killed in front of him, Zedekiah's eyes were put out, and he was led in chains like a slave to Babylon.

On Nebuchadnezzar's orders, the temple and the royal palace and many houses were set on fire, and the city walls razed to the ground. People were rounded up and taken away – only the poor and weak were left behind to scratch what living they could from vineyards and fields.

ISHTAR GATE
This is a detail from the Ishtar Gate, built during King Nebuchadnezzar's reign of Babylon. Its enameled bricks were decorated with lions and bulls.

The Babylonians take possession of Jerusalem and King Zedekiah is led away in chains

Jerusalem is set on fire

The Israelites are rounded up and taken to Babylon

THEY SLEW THE SONS OF ZEDEKIAH BEFORE HIS EYES, AND PUT OUT THE EYES OF ZEDEKIAH, AND BOUND HIM WITH FETTERS OF BRASS, AND CARRIED HIM TO BABYLON.
II KINGS 25:7

The Golden Statue

Shadrach   Meshach   Abednego

King Nebuchadnezzar   Daniel

Daniel tells King Nebuchadnezzar the meaning of his dreams, and in return the king gives Daniel and his three friends important posts

BABYLONIAN EMPIRE
Under Nebuchadnezzar II (605-562 BCE), the Babylonian empire expanded until it dominated the ancient Middle East. The Judeans were one of the peoples that were conquered by the Babylonians and moved far from their homeland.

NEBUCHADNEZZAR, king of Babylon, was tormented by bad dreams. He consulted wise men, astrologers, and magicians, but none could tell him what his dreams conveyed. Eventually the king lost patience, and threatened them all with death, but still none was found who could interpret the terrible image of his nightmare.

Among the wise men was Daniel, a Judean who had been captured by the Babylonians. He was one of a group of young noblemen of exceptional intelligence, strength of character, and good looks who had been chosen for special training. They had been taught the language and history of Babylon, and after three years had been taken into the king's service. With Daniel were three others from Judah who were given new names by their captors: Shadrach, Meshach, and Abednego. The four men soon became good friends. They were all clever and quick to learn, but Daniel had a special gift: he was able to interpret dreams.

Having been sentenced to death with the others, Daniel went to see the king. "Please, sire, let us have more time. I am sure that I will soon be able to tell you the meaning of your dreams," To this Nebuchadnezzar assented, and Daniel and his three friends prayed to God for help. That night God revealed the secret of the king's dream.

Next day, Daniel went again to Nebuchadnezzar. "God has done what your wise men could not, and shown me the meaning of your dreams.

"As you slept, you saw a gigantic statue towering above you. Its head was sculpted of pure gold, its chest and arms of silver, its belly and thighs of bronze, its legs of iron, and its feet part iron, part clay. Suddenly a stone smashed against the statue's feet, and shattered them – whereupon the entire structure, gold, silver, and bronze, crashed to the ground, reduced to nothing but particles of dust. The wind blew the dust away, and the stone became a great mountain that covered the whole earth.

"I will tell you the meaning of this," said Daniel. "The statue's head of gold represents you, great King, and the parts made of silver, bronze, iron, and clay are the empires which shall come after yours, some strong, some weak and easily divided, none lasting forever. The stone is the kingdom of God; it is greater than any kingdom on Earth, and shall never be destroyed."

Nebuchadnezzar was so impressed with Daniel's wisdom that he knelt before him, swearing allegiance to his God. Loading him with treasure, he appointed Daniel governor of Babylon and chief of all his advisers. He also gave important posts to Daniel's friends, Shadrach, Meshach, and Abednego.

Later, the king gave orders for a statue to be built, ninety feet high, nine feet wide, and made of solid gold. He had it set upon the plain of Dura, and with great pomp and ceremony commanded all his officers, governors, captains, and counselors to come and worship the statue as a god. Only Daniel's three friends refused.

When Nebuchadnezzar learned that his order had been defied, he flew into a rage, and demanded that Shadrach, Meshach, and Abednego be brought before him. "If you do not worship as I tell you," shouted the king, "I will have you thrown into a fiery furnace and burnt to death!"

The king orders that a statue made of solid gold be built and commands everyone to worship the statue

THEN NEBUCHADNEZZAR CAME
NEAR TO THE MOUTH OF THE
BURNING FIERY FURNACE, AND
SPAKE, AND SAID, "SHADRACH,
MESHACH, AND ABEDNEGO, YE
SERVANTS OF THE MOST HIGH
GOD, COME FORTH, AND COME
HITHER." THEN SHADRACH,
MESHACH, AND ABEDNEGO
CAME FORTH OF THE MIDST OF
THE FIRE.

DANIEL 3:26

The three men quietly replied, "We will not worship your statue, but our God will save us from the furnace, and protect us even from you, great King. We have nothing to fear."

Nebuchadnezzar, beside himself with rage, had the furnace heated to seven times its usual heat. Then the men, fully clothed, were thrown into the flames. But as he watched, Nebuchadnezzar saw to his astonishment that the three men walked through the fire unharmed, and that beside them stood an unknown fourth man.

"Shadrach, Meshach, and Abednego, come out of the furnace," said the king, his voice full of awe. As they stepped from the flames, everyone saw that not a hair was singed, not a thread of clothing was burnt. Nebuchadnezzar took each in turn by the hand. "From this day, the Jewish people may worship their God, who sent his angel to rescue these men," he vowed. "And I will decree that my people, too, shall worship only your God." Then he embraced the three friends, and gave them positions of great power in the government of Babylon.

The three friends walk through the fire unharmed, while beside them stands an unknown fourth man

King Nebuchadnezzar calls to the three men to come out of the furnace

Belshazzar's Feast

King Belshazzar suddenly sees before him a hand, writing on the plaster of the wall

King Belshazzar

BELSHAZZAR, THE NEW KING OF BABYLON, gave a great feast. He gave orders that the gold and silver cups which his father, Nebuchadnezzar, had plundered from the temple in Jerusalem, should be used as goblets for wine.

As Belshazzar and his friends shouted and laughed and drank toasts to their gods, suddenly they saw before them a hand writing on the white plaster of the wall. The king turned pale, his knees shook, and in a faint voice he called for a wise man to tell him what the words meant. But no one could do so. Then the queen spoke. "Let Daniel be called: he will know what this means."

Daniel looked carefully at the writing on the wall: MENE, MENE, TEKEL, UPHARSIN. He said, "MENE means 'number': the days of your reign are numbered. TEKEL means 'weight': you have been weighed in the moral balance and found wanting. UPHARSIN means 'division': your kingdom will be divided between the Medes and the Persians."

That very night Belshazzar was put to death, and Darius, king of the Medes, took possession of the kingdom of Babylon.

IN THE SAME HOUR CAME FORTH FINGERS OF A MAN'S HAND, AND WROTE OVER AGAINST THE CANDLESTICK UPON THE PLAISTER OF THE WALL OF THE KING'S PALACE: AND THE KING SAW THE PART OF THE HAND THAT WROTE.

DANIEL 5:5

Daniel in the Lions' Den

MEDES
The Medes were closely related to the Persians, and joined forces with them in conquering Babylon. The gold plaque above dates from around 400-300 BCE. It shows a Mede, possibly a priest, dressed in a tunic and trousers and wearing a soft, pointed cap.

Daniel disobeys the new law by continuing to pray to God

DARIUS THE MEDE WAS SO IMPRESSED by the wisdom of Daniel that he appointed him the most powerful man in the kingdom, after himself. This made the other officials jealous, and they plotted to bring about Daniel's downfall. But try as they might, they could find no fault in him. "The only way we can harm him," they said to each other, "is to try and make him do something against the laws of his God."

At their request, Darius issued a ruling that for the next thirty days no one should pray to any god, but only to the king himself. Any man found disobeying the new law would be thrown to the lions.

Daniel heard of this, but continued to pray to God three times a day before his open window, which looked toward Jerusalem and was in full view of the street. His enemies gathered outside to watch, then went off triumphantly to report him to the king.

Darius was dismayed that his favorite, Daniel, should have been made a victim of his law, but there was nothing he could do to save him. With a heavy heart, he gave the order for Daniel to be thrown into the lions' den. "Your God will save you," he said to Daniel, and turned away to hide his sorrow. The entrance was then sealed with a heavy stone. That evening Darius refused both food and drink, and lay all night unable to sleep.

Early the next morning the king hurried to where the lions were penned. "Daniel, Daniel," he called. "Has your God protected you?"

"The Lord sent his angel to stand beside me, and the lions have left me untouched."

Darius was overjoyed, and at once gave the order for Daniel's release. Daniel was lifted out of the lions' den unharmed and unafraid, for he knew that God was with him.

Then Darius had all the conspirators arrested, with their wives, and commanded them to be thrown to the lions. At once the beasts fell on them, savagely tearing them apart until there was nothing left of them but bones.

King Darius

King Darius goes to the lions' den and is overjoyed to find that Daniel is unharmed

MAN-EATING LION
This Phoenician ivory shows a lioness gripping a man by the neck. In the ancient Middle East, people were sometimes executed by being thrown to the lions.

Esther Becomes Queen

Esther comes before King Xerxes, and he chooses her to be his queen

Many young women receive beauty treatments so that the king might choose a new queen

mulberry juice

kohl

henna

COSMETICS
Esther may have used cosmetics such as the ones above. Mulberry juice was used to redden cheeks, kohl to outline the eyes, and henna to color the palms of the hands.

PERFUME MAKING
In ancient times, one way of making perfume was to drop flower petals and seeds into hot olive oil. The oil was strained and then left to cool.

XERXES, ALSO KNOWN AS AHASUERUS, was a powerful king who ruled over the entire Persian empire from India to Ethiopia. In the third year of his reign he gave a great feast, which lasted for over a hundred days. The marble pillars of his palace were hung with silk, and the floors covered in silken carpets, even the beds were made of silver and gold. His guests drank priceless wines from golden goblets studded with jewels.

One night, Xerxes sent for Vashti, his queen, for he wanted to show his guests how beautiful she was. But Vashti refused to appear. At this the king fell into a fury, and gave orders that Vashti should no longer be regarded as his wife. Messengers were sent in every direction to bring to the palace numbers of beautiful maidens so that the king might choose for himself a new queen.

Now in the royal household there was a Jewish man named Mordecai. He had brought up as his own daughter a cousin called Esther, a young girl of outstanding loveliness. When all the candidates were gathered together Esther was among them, and with her sweet nature she soon won favor with the keeper of the women's apartments. Mordecai visited her every day. He impressed on her the importance of never revealing that she was from Judah, for he was afraid that the king would not favor a Jewish girl.

For twelve months the women were tended with the greatest care, bathed in oil of myrrh, massaged with costly creams, their faces expertly painted, their hair brushed until it shone. One by one they were sent in to be inspected by the king. When it came to Esther's turn, he knew he had found the woman he wanted. Without wasting more time, Xerxes married her and crowned her queen.

One day, during the course of his duties, Mordecai overheard two men plotting to assassinate the king. He told Esther; she at once informed her husband, who had the culprits arrested and hanged.

Xerxes made one of his officials, Haman, chief of all his ministers, and commanded his subjects to bow before him. This Mordecai refused to do. Haman, enraged by the man's stubbornness, determined to take his revenge not only on Mordecai but on the entire Jewish people. He told the king that these people were different, they did not obey his laws, and should be destroyed. Xerxes told Haman to deal with them as he wished, and gave him his signet ring. Haman issued an order, sealed with the king's ring, that on an appointed day every Jewish person – man, woman, and child – should be put to death.

Mordecai, appalled and terrified, went to Esther and told her what was planned for their people. He begged her to plead with her husband to spare them. "It is for this purpose that you have become queen."

"Pray for me," said Esther. "I will go to the king, and if I die, I die."

XERXES I
The Persian king who married Esther was Xerxes I, called Ahasuerus in the Bible. His reign lasted from 486-463 BCE. This Persian silver statue, probably of a king, dates from about this time.

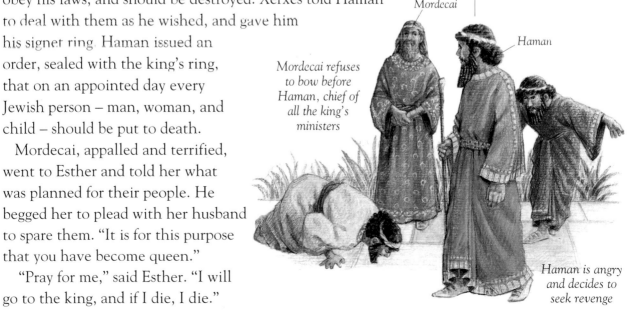

Mordecai

Haman

Mordecai refuses to bow before Haman, chief of all the king's ministers

Haman is angry and decides to seek revenge

Esther Saves Her People

Xerxes, unable to sleep, asks that the book of records be read to him

PRISONERS' FATE
This carving shows Judean prisoners being impaled on stakes. In the Bible it says that Haman was hanged on the gallows. As hanging was not common in Persia, it is possible that Haman met the same fate as these prisoners.

DRESSED IN HER CEREMONIAL ROBES, Esther appeared in the audience hall before the king. From his throne, Xerxes stretched out to her his golden scepter as a sign of favor. "Whatever it is you desire, my queen, shall be yours."

"I ask that you and Haman dine with me tomorrow."

Haman was delighted by the queen's invitation, but meanwhile gave the order to build the gallows from which to hang Mordecai.

Xerxes, meanwhile, could not sleep, and to pass the hours until dawn asked that the book of records be read to him, from which he discovered that Mordecai had never been rewarded for uncovering the plot against his life. "How should I reward a man I wish to honor?" he asked Haman.

Haman, believing the king was referring to himself, replied, "Such a man should be proclaimed a hero. He should be dressed in royal robes, crowned with a golden crown, and led around the city on the king's own horse."

"Then in this way shall I reward Mordecai," said Xerxes, to Haman's dismay.

The next day both the king and Haman dined with Esther, who lost no time in begging a favor of her husband. "Speak, and it shall be granted," said Xerxes fondly.

"My people and I are to be destroyed: we have been bought as slaves, and now we are to be put to death like animals. I implore you to save our lives!"

Xerxes, appalled, demanded to know who was responsible for giving such an order.

"Someone you trusted but who has betrayed your trust," said Esther. "I am speaking of Haman, who is sitting beside you."

Xerxes was so shocked and angry he was unable to say a word. Leaving the table, he strode out into the garden. Haman, completely taken by surprise, went cold with horror. Suddenly realizing the danger he was in, he flung himself at Esther's feet to beg for mercy. The king came back into the room at that same moment, and believing that Haman was attacking his wife, had him arrested. Haman was hanged on the very same gallows that had been built for Mordecai.

Unable to reverse a royal proclamation, Xerxes sent out messengers to every city and province from India to Ethiopia to tell the people that the Jewish people everywhere must be honored and respected, and that they had the right to defend themselves as they saw fit on the day appointed for their destruction. Ever after the Jewish people have celebrated this deliverance, exchanging gifts and giving to the poor.

SCROLL OF ESTHER
The Jewish festival of Purim celebrates the story of Esther. A scroll containing the book of Esther is read in the synagogue. The scroll's case is often ornate, like the silver one above. Every time Haman's name is read, all the people boo and stamp their feet.

Xerxes is shocked and angry to hear what Haman has done

Haman goes cold with horror

Esther accuses Haman of giving the order to destroy her people

The Rebuilding of Jerusalem

King Artaxerxes notices that his cupbearer, Nehemiah, looks unhappy

SILVER CUP
As cupbearer, Nehemiah may have served wine in a silver, horn-shaped cup, such as this one, tasting the wine first to check for poison. A cupbearer held a position of trust, and Nehemiah would have been an influential friend of the king.

SOMETIME EARLIER, Cyrus, king of Persia, had proclaimed that any captive Judeans who wished to return to Judah should be given their freedom. The king had also sent back the silver and gold treasure that had been plundered from the temple by the Babylonians.

The Jewish people who had returned to Jerusalem were saddened to see the state that the city had fallen into – the walls in many places reduced to rubble, the gates blackened by fire. Several of them went to see Nehemiah, cupbearer to Artaxerxes, who was now the king of Persia, to tell him of their damaged city. Nehemiah was so grieved at what he heard that he was unable to hide it from the king while serving wine that evening.

"Why do you look so unhappy?" Artaxerxes inquired. "Are you ill?"

"No, sire," said Nehemiah, "I am not ill, but my heart is breaking because I have been told that Jerusalem, the city of my ancestors, lies in ruins. I beg you to let me go there so that I may start the work of rebuilding." To this Artaxerxes gave his consent, sending with Nehemiah an escort of armed men and letters to the local governors asking them to give him any help he needed.

After Nehemiah had been in Jerusalem for three days, he rode on a donkey by night around the city to see for himself what needed to be repaired. Accompanied by only a few men, he inspected tumbled-down walls and gates that had been half destroyed by fire. Then he summoned the people. "Come, let us rebuild Jerusalem! The condition of our once-great city is a disgrace! Let us pray to God to help us in our work."

Nehemiah gathered together all the volunteers and organized parties of laborers, and gave them directions. But there were some who jeered at his efforts, and threatened to put a stop to the work.

"What do these Israelites think they are doing? Do they really believe that their feeble efforts will make walls out of rubble?"

Some of the men were discouraged, but Nehemiah reassured them.

"Do not be afraid," Nehemiah told his men, "for the Lord is with us, and will protect us." Then he gave spears and shields to half his workforce, and they protected the other half while the repairs were made. And in fifty-two days the work was done.

Nehemiah rides on a donkey by night and inspects the ruined walls of Jerusalem

STONEMASON
Nehemiah would have employed skilled stonemasons to help rebuild Jerusalem. The mason hammered wooden pegs into holes in the rock, then poured water over the pegs. The wood then swelled, causing the stone to split. The mason sawed and trimmed the block with a pick. Stonemasons still practice in parts of the Middle East today.

Jonah and the Great Fish

SPERM WHALE
The "fish" that swallowed Jonah may have been a sperm whale. These whales are known to visit the eastern Mediterranean Sea. With their large throats, they can swallow the body of a man whole.

GOD TOLD HIS PROPHET, Jonah, to go to Nineveh, and warn the people there to turn away from their wickedness. But Jonah disliked the Ninevites and did not want them to hear God's message, so he went instead to Joppa. There he found a berth on a ship sailing to Tarshish. As soon as the ship put out to sea, God sent a great wind that whipped the water up into a storm, and it seemed that the ship would break apart. The sailors, terrified, threw everything they could overboard to lighten the load.

The captain went below, where he found Jonah fast asleep. "Wake up, and pray to your God to save us!" he cried. Meanwhile, the sailors on deck were drawing lots to discover who among them was the cause of the storm. The name drawn was Jonah's.

"Yes," he said. "I am the cause of the trouble. I am an Israelite, and I ran away from the Lord. Throw me over the side, and the storm will die down." At first the men hesitated, and tried to row the ship toward the shore, but the waves grew

The sailors throw Jonah overboard

Jonah is swallowed by a giant fish and for three days and three nights he remained in its belly higher and the wind screamed louder, and they took hold of Jonah and threw him into the sea. At once the wind dropped and the water grew calm.

As Jonah swam in the sea, he was swallowed by a giant fish. For three days and nights he remained in its belly, praying to God and thanking the Lord for keeping him alive, until the fish vomited Jonah onto dry land.

Again the Lord told Jonah to go to Nineveh, and this time he went, and warned the people that their city would be destroyed. The king and all his subjects, knowing that they had done wrong, begged God to spare them and promised that they would mend their ways. God heard their prayers and resolved not to harm them.

Jonah, however, was angry that the city was to be spared.

The fish vomits Jonah onto dry land

As Jonah watches over Nineveh, God makes a vine grow to shade him from the sun, but then causes it to wither and die

He built himself a shelter outside the city walls, meaning to stay there until Nineveh fell. God, watching over him, made a vine grow up to shade Jonah from the sun. But the next morning God sent a worm that fed on the roots of the vine until it withered and died. The sun grew hot, and a stifling wind blew from the east, until Jonah was suffering so much he wished himself dead. "Why are you angry that the vine has withered?" God asked him. "Why do you care about a vine that you neither planted nor watered, while you resent my care for the well-being of a city of thousands of souls?"

NINEVEH
Above is a model of part of the wall that once surrounded Nineveh, the capital of Assyria. The wall was 8 miles (13 km) long. Parks and many grand buildings once lay within these walls.

The Book of Psalms

PSALMS ARE SONGS AND POEMS that praise and honor God. Many are thought to have been written by David, who was a poet, singer, and musician, and was known as the "sweet psalmist of Israel." The psalms cover a wide range of thought and feeling. They praise God as creator, as in psalm 8, and as protector, as in psalm 121 and psalm 23, which compares God to a shepherd, looking after his people in the same way that a shepherd watches over his sheep.

King David is thought to have written many of the psalms

Psalm 8

O Lord our Lord, how excellent is thy name in all the Earth!
Who hast set thy glory above the heavens.
Out of the mouth of babes and sucklings hast thou ordained
strength because of thine enemies,
That thou mightest still the enemy and the avenger.
When I consider thy heavens,
The work of thy fingers,
The moon and the stars,
Which thou hast ordained;
What is man, that thou art mindful of him?
And the son of man, that thou visitest him?
For thou hast made him a little lower than the angels,
And hast crowned him with glory and honor.
Thou madest him to have dominion over the works of thy hands;
Thou hast put all things under his feet,
All sheep and oxen,
Yea, and the beasts of the field;
The fowl of the air, and the fish of the sea,
And whatsoever passeth through the paths of the seas.
O Lord our Lord, how excellent is thy name in all the Earth!

Psalm 23

The Lord is my shepherd; I shall not want.
He maketh me to lie down in green pastures,
He leadeth me beside the still waters.
He restoreth my soul.
He leadeth me in the paths of righteousness for his name's sake.
Yea, though I walk through the valley of the shadow of death,
I will fear no evil, for thou art with me;
Thy rod and thy staff they comfort me.
Thou preparest a table before me in the presence of mine enemies,
Thou anointest my head with oil;
My cup runneth over.
Surely goodness and mercy shall follow me all the days of my life,
And I will dwell in the house of the Lord forever.

THE LORD IS MY SHEPHERD;
I SHALL NOT WANT. HE
MAKETH ME TO LIE DOWN IN
GREEN PASTURES.
PSALMS 23:1-2

Psalm 121

I will lift up mine eyes unto the hills,
From whence cometh my help.
My help cometh from the Lord,
Which made Heaven and Earth.
He will not suffer thy foot to be moved,
He that keepeth thee will not slumber.
Behold, he that keepeth Israel shall neither slumber nor sleep.
The Lord is thy keeper: the Lord is thy shade upon thy right hand.
The sun shall not smite thee by day, nor the moon by night.
The Lord shall keep thee from all evil,
He shall keep thy soul.
The Lord shall guard thy going out,
And thy coming in from this time forth,
And even forevermore.

Psalm 23 compares God to a shepherd

Who's Who in the Bible Stories

Aaron and Moses ask Pharaoh to let their people go, but Pharaoh refuses

AARON Moses' brother, who was his spokesman when they met Pharaoh. *Pages 71, 72-73, 74, 84-85, 90-91*

ABEDNEGO One of Daniel's three friends. *Pages 162-164*

ABEL Adam and Eve's second son and Cain's brother. *Pages 22-23*

ABIGAIL King David's wife. *Pages 124-125*

ABRAHAM/ABRAM The first Patriarch of the Israelites. His faith in God made him a great leader. *Pages 30-44*

ABSALOM King David's son. *Pages 132-133*

ADAM The first man. *Pages 20-21, 24*

AHAB A king of Israel who lived at the time of Elijah. *Pages 142-145*

ARTAXERXES The Persian king who allowed the cupbearer, Nehemiah, to return to Jerusalem. *Page 172*

BALAAM A prophet called upon to curse the Israelites. *Pages 86-87*

BALAK The king of the Moabites who asked Balaam to curse the Israelites. *Pages 86-87*

BATHSHEBA King David's wife and Solomon's mother. *Pages 130-131, 133*

BELSHAZZAR The king of Babylon who saw mysterious writing on the wall during a feast. *Page 165*

BENJAMIN The youngest son of Jacob and Rachel. *Pages 30, 62-65*

BOAZ A Bethlehem farmer who married Ruth. *Pages 106-107*

CAIN The first son of Adam and Eve. He murdered his brother Abel. *Pages 22-23*

CALEB One of the spies sent to find out about the promised land. *Page 90*

CYRUS The king of Babylon during whose reign the Israelites went back to Jerusalem. *Pages 153, 172*

DANIEL An Israelite who rose to an important position in Babylon. He had a gift for interpreting dreams. *Pages 162-167*

DARIUS A king of the Medes who ruled Babylon. *Pages 165, 166, 167*

DAVID The Bethlehem shepherd boy who became a king of Israel. *Pages 117, 116-125, 128-133, 135, 176*

DELILAH A Philistine woman who betrayed the secret of Samson's strength. *Pages 102-103*

EBED-MELECH The servant who rescued Jeremiah from the pit. *Page 160*

ELI The high priest who raised Samuel. *Pages 108-110*

ELIJAH A great prophet of Israel who had a contest with the priests of Baal. *Pages 140-146*

ELISHA The man who followed Elijah as God's prophet. *Pages 146-151*

ESAU Jacob's twin brother and the son of Isaac and Rebekah. *Pages 46-48, 54-55*

ESTHER The young Jewish queen in the court of King Xerxes who prevented the massacre of the Jewish people. *Pages 168-171*

King Xerxes chooses Esther to be his queen

EVE The first woman. *Pages 20-22*

GEHAZI Elisha's servant. *Pages 147-149*

GIDEON A judge who defeated the Midianites with a few soldiers. *Pages 96-97*

David's stone strikes Goliath on the forehead and kills him

GOLIATH The great Philistine soldier killed by David. *Pages 118-119*

HAGAR The servant of Sarah and the mother of Ishmael. *Pages 34-35, 40-41*

HAM One of Noah's three sons. *Page 24*

HAMAN The man whose murderous plot Esther stopped. *Pages 169-171*

HANNAH Samuel's mother. *Page 108*

HEZEKIAH A king of Judah during the time of Isaiah. *Page 155*

HULDAH Prophetess at the time of Josiah. *Page 156*

ISAAC Son of Abraham and Sarah and the father of Jacob and Esau. *Pages 30-31, 35, 40, 42-48*

ISAIAH A prophet who foretold the coming of the Messiah. *Pages 154-155*

ISHMAEL Son of Abraham and Hagar, Sarah's servant. *Pages 35, 40-41*

ISRAEL The name later given to Jacob and his descendants. *Pages 31, 55*

JACOB One of Isaac's sons who stole Esau's inheritance. Father of the 12 tribes of Israel. *Pages 30-31, 46-55, 56, 62-65*

JAPHETH One of Noah's three sons. *Page 24*

JEPHTHAH A general who sacrificed his daughter because of a vow he made. *Pages 98-99*

JEREMIAH A prophet in Judah who foretold great misfortunes. *Pages 158-161*

JESSE King David's father. *Pages 116-117*

JETHRO Moses' father-in-law. *Pages 70, 72*

JEZEBEL Ahab's cruel wife. *Pages 144-145*

JOAB The commander of King David's army. *Pages 131, 133*

JONAH The prophet whose disobedience led to his being swallowed by a great fish. *Pages 174-175*

JONATHAN The son of King Saul who became David's close friend. *Pages 120, 122-123, 127*

JOSEPH Jacob's favorite son. He was sold into slavery in Egypt, then rose to a position of power. *Pages 30, 53, 56-65, 89*

JOSHUA The leader of the Israelites after Moses. *Pages 91, 93-95*

JOSIAH A man who became king of Judah at a young age. *Pages 156-157*

JUDAH One of Jacob's 12 sons. *Pages 30, 57, 64-65*

LABAN Rebekah's brother. Father of Rachel and Leah. *Pages 30, 45, 48, 51-53, 54*

LEAH Daughter of Laban and Jacob's wife. *Pages 51-53*

LOT Abraham's nephew who lived in Sodom. *Pages 32-33, 37-39, 98*

MESHACH One of Daniel's three friends. *Pages 162-164*

MICHAL Saul's daughter who became David's wife. *Pages 120-121, 129*

MIRIAM The sister of Moses and Aaron. *Page 78*

MORDECAI The cousin of Esther. *Pages 169-171*

MOSES The man who led the Israelites out of Egypt to search for the promised land. *Pages 67-85, 90-92*

NAAMAN An army general whose leprosy was healed by Elisha. *Pages 150-151*

NABAL Abigail's husband. *Pages 124-125*

NABOTH A farmer who was killed for his vineyard by King Ahab. *Pages 144-145*

NAOMI The mother-in-law of the devoted Ruth. *Pages 106-107*

NATHAN The prophet who delivered God's word to David. *Page 131*

NEBUCHADNEZZAR The king of Babylon who captured Jerusalem and took the people of Judah into exile. *Pages 152, 159, 161-164*

Samson kills a lion, tearing it apart with his hands

NEHEMIAH After the Jewish exile in Babylon, he returned to rebuild Jerusalem. *Pages 172-173*

NOAH He and his family were saved from death in the great flood by building a boat. *Pages 24-27*

ORPAH Naomi's daughter-in-law. *Page 106*

POTIPHAR The Egyptian courtier for whom Joseph worked. *Pages 58-59*

RACHEL Jacob's favorite wife. The mother of Joseph and Benjamin. *Pages 30, 50-53, 56*

RAHAB A Jericho woman who hid two Israelite spies in her house. *Pages 93, 95*

REBEKAH Isaac's wife, the mother of Jacob and Esau. *Pages 30, 44-48*

REHOBOAM Solomon's son, who caused the kingdom to be split in two. *Pages 89, 140*

REUBEN Jacob's eldest son. *Pages 30, 57*

RUTH The devoted daughter-in-law of Naomi, who traveled with her to Bethlehem. *Pages 106-107*

SAMSON An Israelite man of great strength who fought against the Philistines. *Pages 100-105*

SAMUEL The prophet who annointed Saul and David, Israel's first two kings. *Pages 108-109, 112-113, 115-117, 126-127*

SARAH/SARAI Abraham's wife and the mother of Isaac. *Pages 32-36, 40*

SATAN The name sometimes given to the devil, who is thought to be the source of all sin and evil. *Page 20*

SAUL The first king of Israel. *Pages 89, 112-115, 118-123, 126-127*

SENNACHERIB King of Assyria whose army trapped Hezekiah in Jerusalem. *Pages 152, 155*

SHADRACH One of Daniel's three friends. *Pages 162-164*

SHAPMAN Scribe to Josiah. *Page 155*

SHEBA, QUEEN OF The queen who visited Solomon. *Pages 138-139*

SHEM One of Noah's three sons. *Page 24*

SOLOMON King David's son. The king who built the Temple in Jerusalem. *Pages 132, 134-139*

URIAH Bathsheba's husband who was sent to his death by King David. *Pages 130-131*

VASHTI The queen who Xerxes deposed. *Page 168*

XERXES The Persian king who married Esther. Also known as Ahasuerus. *Pages 168-171*

ZEDEKIAH The last king of Judah. *Pages 159-161*

The Babylonians take possession of Jerusalem, and King Zedekiah is led away in chains

Places in the Bible Stories

Set out below are famous places of the Old Testament where important events took place For each entry, there is a brief description of what happened there and who was involved, followed by the page references where the place name appears in the main text, captions, or on maps.

ARABIA Ishmaelite traders carried goods from Arabia to Egypt; on one such trip, they bought Joseph for twenty pieces of silver from his brothers, then sold him to one of Pharoah's officers. *Pages 32, 57, 153*

ARABIAN DESERT East of the land of Moab. *Pages 15, 48, 70, 86, 140, 162*

ASHER One of the original 12 kingdoms of Israel. *Page 89*

ASSUR The Assyrians worshiped at the temple here. *Pages 152-153*

ASSYRIA An ancient country traditionally at war with Israel. *Pages 14, 48, 89, 137, 152-153*

BABEL Traditionally, Babel was thought to be Babylon, where the Tower of Babel was built. *Pages 15, 28-29*

BABYLON Centuries after the flood, Noah's descendants built the great Tower of Babel in this ancient walled city, the capital of the empire of Babylonia. After Jerusalem was sacked, the Israelites were taken here as captives. Where Daniel's three friends walked through a fiery furnace and survived, King Belshazzar saw the writing on the wall, and Daniel was thrown to the lions. *Pages 15, 28-29, 32, 89, 152-153, 159, 161-166*

BABYLONIA Situated between the southern reaches of the Tigris and Euphrates rivers, this ancient country defeated the Assyrians. *Pages 15, 28-29, 152-153*

BEERSHEBA (desert) When Hagar and her son Ishmael wandered into the wilderness, an angel appeared to show her where there was a spring, so they were able to have water to drink. For some years, they made their home in this desert. *Pages 32, 40-41*

BEERSHEBA (town) Abraham first settled here at the end of his journey to Canaan. Later, his grandson Jacob played a trick on his brother Esau and was forced to leave home. *Pages 15, 31, 42, 43, 46-48*

BEN HINNOM The valley where Jeremiah smashed a potter's clay jar and predicted that God would destroy the wicked Judeans. *Page 158*

BENJAMIN One of the original 12 kingdoms of Israel. *Page 89*

BETHEL ("the house of God") Jacob stopped here on his journey to Haran from Beersheba. God appeared to him in a dream of a stairway reaching up to heaven, with angels moving up and down it. *Pages 15, 31, 48-50, 89, 146*

BETHLEHEM When widowed, Naomi journeyed back here to her own country, with the devoted Ruth. The birthplace of David, who was later anointed by Samuel as the next king of the Israelites. *Pages 15, 89, 106*

BROOK OF KERITH Elijah secretly lived near the brook, which God ensured had plenty of water for drinking. *Pages 15, 140*

CANAAN ("the promised land") Abraham and his people settled here, after traveling from Ur. His grandson Jacob lived in this land with his twelve sons. During the great famine, Jacob sent ten of his sons to Egypt to buy wheat. The Israelites settled here, after forty years in the wilderness. Later, the kingdom was divided into two: Israel in the north and Judah in the south. *Pages 15, 30, 32-33, 35, 42, 44, 45, 48, 54, 56, 62-63, 86, 88-91, 98, 100, 103, 133*

The Jezreel valley (shown here) is in the northern part of Canaan

DAMASCUS Jacob passed through here on his way to Haran. *Pages 48, 162*

DAN One of the original 12 kingdoms of Israel. *Pages 89, 91*

The Dead Sea contains so much salt that nothing can live there

DEAD SEA The River Jordan flows into the Dead Sea, situated in southern Canaan. *Pages 15, 38, 39, 86, 89, 123, 140, 151*

EDOM A country to the south of Moab. *Page 15, 86*

EGYPT Joseph was taken here by Ishmaelite traders, after he was sold by his brothers for twenty pieces of silver. Joseph interpreted the Pharoah's dreams and predicted a famine. Joseph was made Governor of Egypt and was able to encourage his family to move here from Canaan during the famine. God and Moses inflicted ten plagues on Egypt before the Pharaoh would allow the Israelites to leave. *Pages 15, 31, 32, 41, 56-78, 84, 91, 135, 139, 153*

ENDOR The witch at Endor summoned up the spirit of Samuel to tell Saul he would be defeated by the Philistines. *Page 126*

EN-GEDI David hid in a cave near here, when Saul and his men were trying to kill him. *Pages 15, 89, 123*

EPHRAIM One of the original 12 kingdoms of Israel. *Page 89*

"FERTILE CRESCENT" A strip of land which stretched from Egypt, through Canaan and Mesopotamia, to Babylonia. *Page 14*

GAD One of the original 12 kingdoms of Israel. *Page 89*

GARDEN OF EDEN Adam and Eve first lived here, before eating the fruit of the Tree of Knowledge. *Pages 20-21*

GATH The place where Goliath lived, but he was defeated by David. *Page 118*

GAZA After being tricked by Delilah, Samson was blinded and thrown into prison here. When his hair grew back he managed to destroy the temple and everyone in it, including himself. *Pages 102-105*

GILEAD Situated in the promised land of Canaan. *Page 91*

GOSHEN Joseph's family and friends were given land in Goshen when they moved to Egypt to escape from the famine in Canaan. *Pages 15, 66-67*

HARAN This was the first stop for Abraham on his way to Canaan, and later on he and his wife Sarai settled here. Here also, Jacob met and married his cousins Rachel and Leah. *Pages 15, 30, 31, 32, 48, 50-53, 162*

HEBRON The town where the Israelites proclaimed the new king David. *Pages 15, 89, 128*

HEZEKIAH'S TUNNEL Built beneath Jerusalem, to ensure the city's water supply, when the Assyrians attacked and carried off the king's gold. *Page 155*

ISHTAR GATE Built during King Nebuchadnezzar's reign of Babylon, as entrance to the Hanging Gardens. *Pages 152-153, 161*

ISRAEL The Bible first used this word to describe Jacob as "the one who fights for God," but eventually it meant the land where Jacob's descendants lived, and was divided into 12 kingdoms. Samuel anointed Saul as the first king of Israel. Later, Israel was the kingdom in the north, Judah in the south. After 200 years, the Assyrians destroyed Israel. *Pages 16, 30, 31, 68-69, 88-91, 100, 112, 120, 132, 135, 139, 140, 142, 150-153*

ISSACHAR One of the original 12 kingdoms of Israel. *Page 89*

JABESH Saul and the Israelite army defeated the Ammonites and freed the city of Jabesh. *Page 114*

JERICHO During the Battle of Jericho, God asked that on the seventh day the Israelite

army walk around the city seven times, the priests blow their trumpets, and the people shout to the skies. Then the walls of Jericho fell to the ground, killing everyone except for Rahab and her family.
Pages 15, 86, 89, 91, 93-95

Jerusalem became the Israelites' political and religious center

JERUSALEM David brought the Ark of the Covenant here, which he made the capital of Israel. He fell in love and married Bathsheba in this city. Near here, David's son Absalom was caught by his long hair in the branches of an oak tree and Joab killed him. Later, King Solomon built a temple here to house the Ark of the Covenant. The Queen of Sheba visited to learn about Solomon's wisdom. The city became the capital of Judah, after Israel split in two. Here also, the prophet Isaiah had a vision. Later, the Babylonians destroyed the city. *Pages 15, 17, 42, 89, 128, 130, 132, 135, 136, 138, 140, 153-157, 159, 162, 165, 166, 172*

JEZREEL VALLEY Saul died in this valley in northern Canaan, overlooked by Mount Gilboa. *Pages 15, 91, 127, 143, 148*

JORDAN An area southeast of Moab. *Pages 15, 33*

JUDAH One of the original 12 kingdoms of Israel, later a country in its own right. Ruled by Solomon's descendants, beginning with his son Rehoboam, but was taken over by the Babylonians more than 300 years later. *Pages 15, 89-91, 140, 152-153, 156, 158, 159, 162, 168, 172*

KIDRON VALLEY Where the Israelites burnt their altars and statues to false gods. *Page 157*

LACHISH A city in Israel captured by the Assyrians. *Pages 152-153*

LAKE HULEH Where the River Jordan began in the north, to flow down to the Sea of Galilee. *Page 151*

LEBANON Cedarwood from Lebanon's hills was used to build Solomon's temple. *Pages 15, 89, 136*

MANASSEH One of the original 12 kingdoms of Israel. *Page 89*

MEDITERRANEAN SEA Most of the events of the Old Testament took place in a small area east of the Mediterranean Sea. *Pages 14, 32, 67, 70, 78, 89, 140, 143, 153, 162, 174*

MESOPOTAMIA Ancient country situated between the upper reaches of the Tigris and Euphrates rivers. *Pages 15, 32, 33, 44, 50*

MIDIAN Moses arrived here after fleeing from Egypt. The people of Midian (Midianites) were the powerful enemy of the Israelites. *Pages 15, 70, 72, 96-97*

MOAB Balak, the king of the Moabites, felt threatened when, during their Exodus, the Israelites camped on the plains of the land of Moab. Also, Naomi made her home here until she was widowed. *Pages 15, 86, 106*

MORIAH After leaving his home in Beersheba and journeying through the Negev Desert, Abraham reached the land of Moriah where he intended to sacrifice his beloved son Isaac. Instead, God's angel let him save Isaac and instead sacrifice a ram caught in a thicket. *Pages 31, 42-43*

MOUNT ARARAT After the great flood, when it rained for forty days and forty nights, Noah's Ark came to rest on a mountain peak in Ararat (now part of Turkey). *Pages 14, 26-27*

MOUNT CARMEL David met his future wife Abigail in a ravine here. Elijah built an altar to God here, so that the rains would come after a long drought. *Pages 15, 34-35, 40-41, 89, 124-125, 140, 142-143, 148*

MOUNT GILBOA The setting in northern Canaan of the horrific battle where the Philistines defeated the Israelites, and Saul died. *Pages 15, 89, 127, 148*

MOUNT HOREB Another name for Mount

Sinai, as it was sometimes called in the Bible. *Page 83*

MOUNT NEBO Situated in the northern part of the kingdom of Reuben. *Pages 15, 67, 86, 89*

MOUNT PISGAH After forty years of wandering in the wilderness, Moses climbed to the summit of Mount Pisgah, where God showed him the whole of the promised land of Canaan. There, Moses died and was buried. *Page 91*

MOUNT SINAI While tending his sheep, Moses heard God speak to him from a burning bush and ask that Moses bring his people out of Egypt. After three months of wandering, the Israelites camped at the foot of the holy mountain of Sinai. Here, God gave to Moses the laws which his people were to follow: the Ten Commandments. When Moses returned, he saw that his people were worshiping a Golden Calf, which made God very angry. *Pages 15, 16, 70-71, 82-84*

NAHOR A city in Mesopotamia, where Abraham's servant found Rebekah at the well outside the city gates. She offered water to him and his camels, and returned with the servant to marry Abraham's son Isaac. *Pages 44-45*

NAPHTALI One of the original 12 kingdoms of Israel. *Page 89*

NEGEV DESERT Siutated in southern Canaan. *Pages 15, 31, 42, 140*

NIMRUD A city in Assyria. *Page 137*

NINEVEH The capital of Assyria. When Jonah ran away from here and traveled on a ship from Joppa to Tarshish, he was swallowed by a great fish. *Pages 15, 152-153, 155, 162, 174-175*

NOD After Cain killed Abel, he came to live in the land of Nod, which is to the east of Eden. *Page 23*

PARAN DESERT Moses camped here and sent twelve men to spy out Canaan. *Page 90*

PERSIA An ancient empire as far east as India and south to Ethiopia. Esther became Queen of Persia, when she married King Xerxes. *Pages 32-33, 37-39, 98, 153, 162, 168-172*

PETHOR Balaam, a fortune-teller, lived here by the River Euphrates. *Page 87*

PITHOM This Egyptian city was built by Israelite slaves. *Page 67*

PLAIN OF DURA A golden statue was built here, but Daniel's friends refused to worship it. *Page 163*

RAMESES The Israelite slaves left this Egyptian city, built by themselves, to follow Moses during the Exodus. *Pages 15, 67, 78,*

RED SEA In the story of the Exodus, God divided this narrow body of water so that the Israelites could escape from the Egyptian army. *Pages 15, 67, 70, 75, 78-79*

REUBEN One of the original 12 kingdoms of Israel. *Page 89*

RIVERS EUPHRATES AND TIGRIS The two major rivers running through the countries of Babylonia and Mesopotamia. *Pages 15, 32, 48, 87, 153, 162*

RIVER JABBOK On his return journey to Beersheba with his family, Jacob crossed the river then fought with God all night. In the morning, God gave him the name of "Israel." *Pages 15, 54-55*

RIVER JORDAN Joshua led his people to the River Jordan, which was all that divided them from the promised land. It stopped flowing, while their priests carried the Ark of the Covenant across it. After they settled in Canaan, the Israelites grew many crops in the river valley. Later, Elijah beat the river's surface and the waters divided. Where Elisha sent the Syrian Naaman to heal himself of leprosy. *Pages 54, 88, 93, 94, 146, 150-151*

RIVER NILE Egypt's Pharoah stood by this river and had a strange dream about a

The River Nile was ancient Egypt's greatest asset

seven-year famine. When a new Pharoah decreed that any male child born to an Israelite woman would be put to death, one such mother hid her baby Moses in the bulrushes. He was found by the Pharoah's daughter who later adopted him. Later, Moses waited on the banks of the Nile for Pharaoh to answer whether he would let the Israelites leave Egypt. When the Pharaoh refused, God helped Moses inflict ten plagues on Egypt. *Pages 15, 60, 62, 66-69, 73-74, 153*

SAMARIA Became the capital of Israel, after the country split in two. Where King Ahab had his palace next to the vineyard of Naboth, who was tricked by Jezebel. *Pages 15, 89, 140, 142, 144, 151*

SEA OF GALILEE Situated in the south of the kingdom of Naphtali. From here, the River Jordan flowed down to the Dead Sea. *Pages 15, 89, 140, 151*

SHEBA A country in southwestern Arabia from where its Queen traveled to Jerusalem to learn about the wisdom of Solomon. *Pages 138-139*

SHILOH Hannah and her husband Elkanah went there to pray. Her prayers were answered when she gave birth to a son, Samuel. Later, the Philistines stole the Ark of the Covenant from its home here. *Pages 15, 89*

SHINAR The earlier biblical name for Babylonia. *Pages 28-29*

SHUNEM Elisha foretold that the woman of Shunem (now called Solem) would give birth to a boy. Later he used his staff to bring the boy back to life when he died. *Pages 15, 147-149*

SIDON Where Elijah brought a woman's son back to life. *Pages 15, 140-141*

SIMEON One of the original 12 kingdoms of Israel. *Page 89*

SINAI DESERT During the time the Israelites wandered here after leaving Egypt, God helped Moses care for them and provided manna from Heaven, flocks of quails, and water from a rock. *Pages 15, 67, 69, 80-81*

SODOM and GOMMORAH (southeastern end of the Dead Sea) Lot finally settled in Sodom at the end of Abraham's journey to the promised land. When God rained down fire and brimstone on these two cities because their inhabitants were guilty of terrible crimes, God forewarned Lot so he and his family fled to Zoar. *Pages 15, 31-33, 37-39*

Gideon chose men for battle at the Spring of Harod (shown above)

SPRING OF HAROD The place where Gideon took his men to drink before the battle with the Midianites, and chose those who were to fight with him. *Pages 96-97*

SUCCOTH Moses and the Israelites passed through this place, during the Exodus to the Red Sea. *Pages 15, 78*

SYRIA Silver items were exported from Syria to Egypt. *Pages 32, 48, 51-53, 65, 140, 150-151, 162*

TIMNAH The place where Samson fought with a lion and killed it. Later, he married a beautiful Philistine woman who lived there. *Page 101*

TOB The land where Jepthah, son of Gilead, went to live after his brothers turned him out of the house. *Page 98*

TYRE Hiram, the king of Tyre, supplied cedarwood to Solomon for building his temple. *Pages 15, 136*

UGARIT (now Ras Sharma in Syria) A statue of Baal, worshiped by the Canaanites, was found here. *Page 88*

UR (in Mesopotamia) Birthplace of Abraham, who left here with his family to travel to the promised land of Canaan. *Pages 15, 29-32, 162*

ZEBULUN One of the original 12 kingdoms of Israel. *Page 89*

ZOAR Just before reaching the safety of Zoar, Lot's wife looked back at the destruction of Sodom and Gomorrah and was turned into a pillar of salt. *Pages 38-39*

INDEX

Acknowledgments

Picture Credits

l=left, r=right, t=top, c=center, b-bottom

Ancient Art & Architecture Collection: 60tl.

Ardea: /Wardene Weisser: 80tl.

ASAP: /Aliza Auerbach 14b, 16ltr; /Israel Talby 88b.

A-Z Botanical Collection: 136tl.

Barnaby's Picture Library: 54bl.

BBC Radio Vision: 10br, 11tl.

Bijbels Museum, Amsterdam, 1992: 108tl.

Bridgeman Art Library: Whitford and Hughes 8-9; Royal Library Stockholm 10tl.

British Library: 9c.

Trustees of the British Museum: 11c, 20bl, 32tl, 32tr, 33t, 64, 68tl, 68bl, 69tr, 73br, 87br, 103tr, 137br, 144bl, 146bl, 154br, 160cl, 166tl, 167br, 168tr.

Peter Clayton: 65tr.

Bruce Coleman Ltd: 175br.

Professor A. Danin, Jerusalem: 80cl.

Mary Evans Picture Library: 26tl.

Chris Fairclough: 93cr.

Werner Forman Archive: 62tl.

Giraudon: 59br.

Sonia Halliday Photographs: 17bc, 31b, 43tr, 78bl, 83tr, 91br, 95tr, 97tr, 102bl, 107tl, 117tr, 127tr, 135tr, 147tr, 151tr, 155tr, 156bl, 157br, 158tl.

Hamburger Kunsthalle: 51t.

Robert Harding Picture Library: 15bl, 29tr, 50b, 53tr, 59tr, 61cr, 63cr, 72cl, 76bl, 111tr, 123cr, 148bl, 174tl.

Michael Holford: 58bl, 73tr, 84tl, 132bl, 152b.

Hutchison Picture Library: 11b, 33br, 34tl, 35tr, 51b, 125cr, 139br; /Sarah Errington 52bl.

Image Bank: 128tl; /F. Roiter 131tr; /J. L. Stage 108bl.

Israel Museum, Jerusalem: 11tr; /The Shrine of the Book, D. Samuel & Jeane H. Gottman Center for Biblical Manuscripts 171tr.

Kunsthistorisches Vienna © Mayer: 66t.

Erich Lessing Archive: 101cr, 150bl, 170bl, 172bl.

Life File: 149tr.

NHPA: /Anthony Bannister 20tl.

Oriental Institute, Chicago: /John Hudson 159br.

Oxford Scientific Films: 45tr.

Planet Earth: /Richard Coomber 141br; /Peter Stephenson 46tl.

Dino Politis: 25br, 29br, 87tr, 173tr.

Zev Radovan: 23tr, 24tl, 27tr, 39br, 40br, 41tr, 98tl, 119br, 130bl, 133br, 142tl, 143br.

Scala: 40tr.

Spectrum Colour Library: 106bl.

Sheila Weir: 45tr.

ZEFA: 17br, 42tl, 42bl, 44bl, 66bc, 128bl.

Dorling Kindersley would like to thank:

Marion Dent for compiling Who's Who in the Bible Stories and Places in the Bible. Tim Ridley, Nick Goodall, and Gary Ombler at the DK Studio; Dorian Spencer Davies; Antonio Forcione; Sally Geeve; Christopher Gillingwater; Polly Goodman; George Hart; Alan Hills; James W. Hunter; Robin Hunter; Marcus James; Fran Jones; Anna Kunst; Michelle de Larrabeiti; Antonio Montoro; Anderley Moore; Jackie Ogburn; Derek Peach; Lenore Person; Dino Politis; Becky Smith; Lara Tankel Holtz; and Martin Wilson for their help in producing this book.

Picture research: Diana Morris, Julia Harris-Voss

Index: Lynn Bresler